Table of Contents

TRADEMARKS AND COPYRIGHT

AirsoftPRESS.com (a.k.a. AirsoftPRESS) is an independent content developer. We at AirsoftPRESS are not associated nor affiliated with the firearm/airsoft replica manufacturer(s) mentioned in this book. The name(s), model(s) and other specific properties of the firearm(s)/replica(s) mentioned in this book are the trademark(s) of the respective manufacturer(s). We mention these name(s) and/or the relevant terminologies only for describing the relevant Airsoft technical knowledge (i.e. Fair Use).

Our publications are fully copyrighted. Unauthorized re-production or duplication are strictly prohibited.

AirsoftPRESS will not be held liable for any advice or suggestions given in this book. If the reader wants to follow a suggestion, it is at his or her own discretion. Suggestions are only offered to help.

ABOUT THE REAL STEEL

The KG9 (and its variants such as TEC-9, MP-9 ...etc) has its origins in Sweden, originally designed by Interdynamic AB. It is an open bolt semi-automatic pistol made of molded polymers and a mixture of stamped and milled steel parts.

PREFACE

This training book has been developed from the ground up for beginners who know little about Airsoft AEG technology. As part of our Airsoft Technology Self-Paced Training Series, this book gives an introduction to the KG9 SMG AEG architecture. The primary goal of this book is to explain the various technical concepts in very simple language.

* We use the Echo1 GAT KG9 implementation for demonstration.

We believe that this book and its support materials have everything you need for an informative, interesting, challenging and entertaining Airsoft educational experience.

BASIC CONCEPT OF THE KG9 SMG DESIGN

The heart of every KG9 SMG AEG is the gearbox. The motor drives the gearbox. The gearbox is like an automatic pump which pumps out air for propelling bullets.

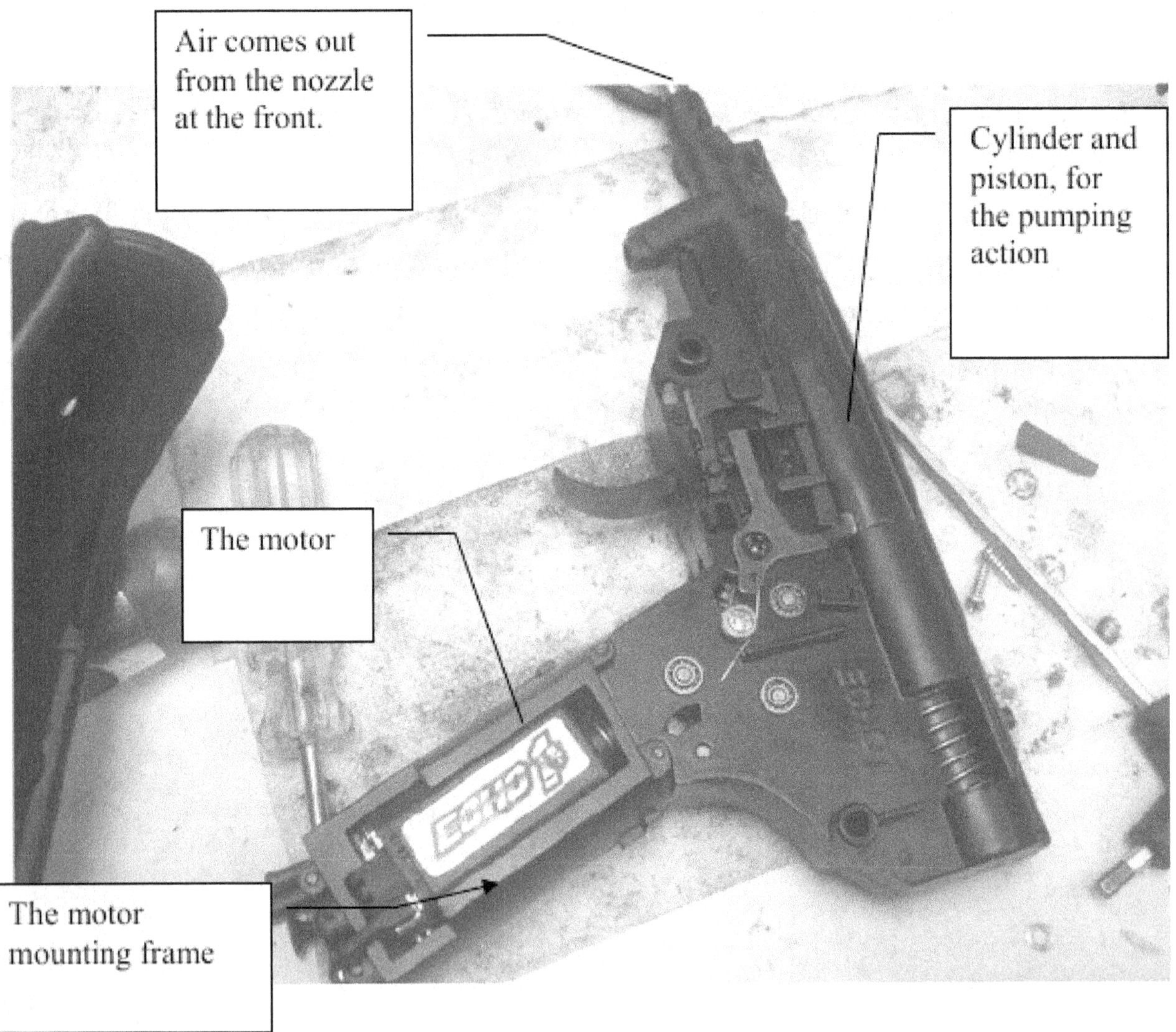

The gearbox is unique but the internals are mostly compatible with the standard gearbox designs.

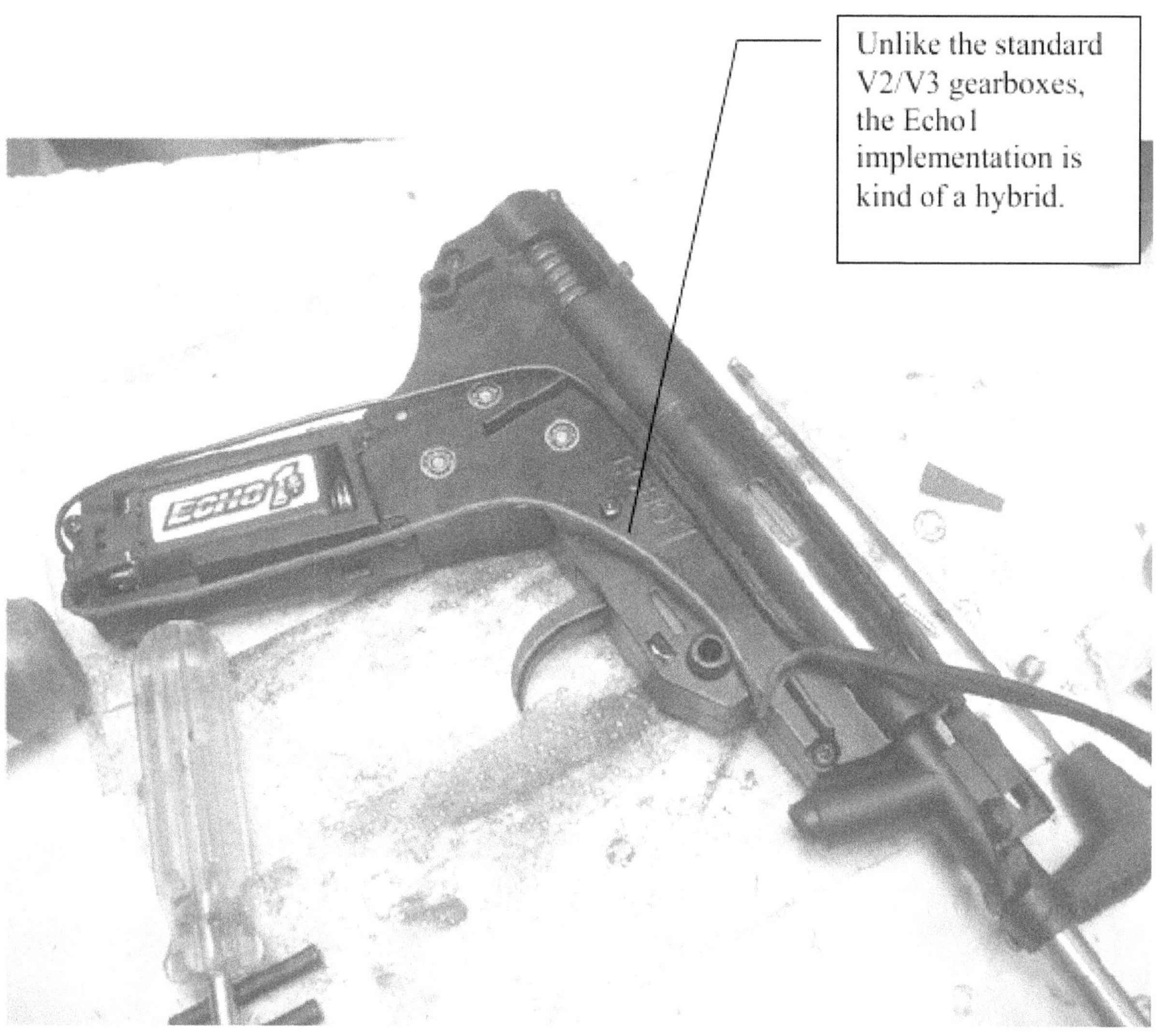

Do note that this gearbox is NOT blowback capable. There is also no recoil shock effect. Some other KG9 AEGs in the market have implemented simple blowback. The Echo1 version does not.

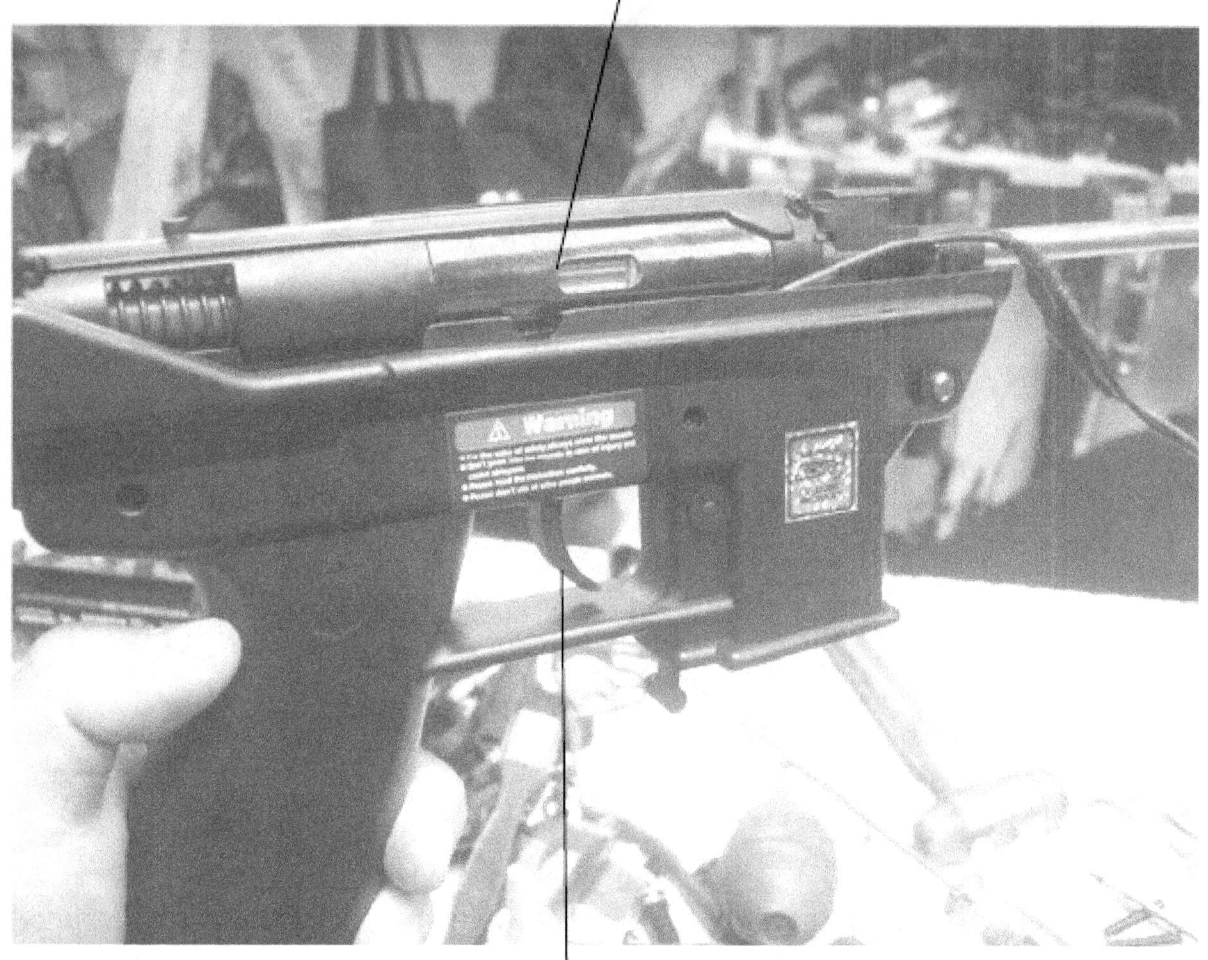

The gearbox sits on the plastic receiver.

The gearbox has the trigger unit attached.

The gearbox comes with 8mm ball bearings:

Ball bearings use small metal balls as the rollers. When the load is transmitted from the outer race to the balls (and then from the ball to the inner race), the balls only contact the inner and outer race at very small points, meaning there isn't much contact area holding the load. When the bearings are overloaded, the balls can deform or squish. The smaller the balls, the weaker they are.

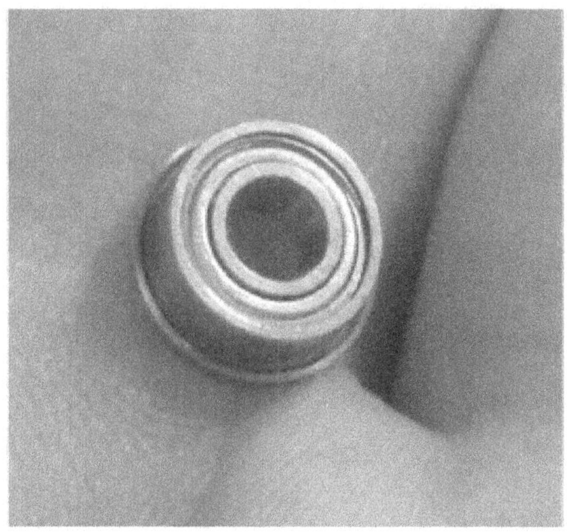

Bearings need to be properly maintained. If you spray silicon oil (or other contact cleaner, such as the Trinity Motor Blast Spray) onto it you can flush away dirt and may also flush away the bearing oil. So you will need to have spare bearing oil with you. I don't think it is really necessary to open up the bearing for oil filling. Just add a few drops onto one side of the bearing and the oil will slowly fill in.

Bearing oil can be purchased from your local hardware shop. It is NOT the same as gear grease so you need to make it very clear to the shop attendant that the oil is for use on ball bearings.

3 gears inside. The motor drives the gear train.

The gears are the same as the standard V2/ V3 based gears.

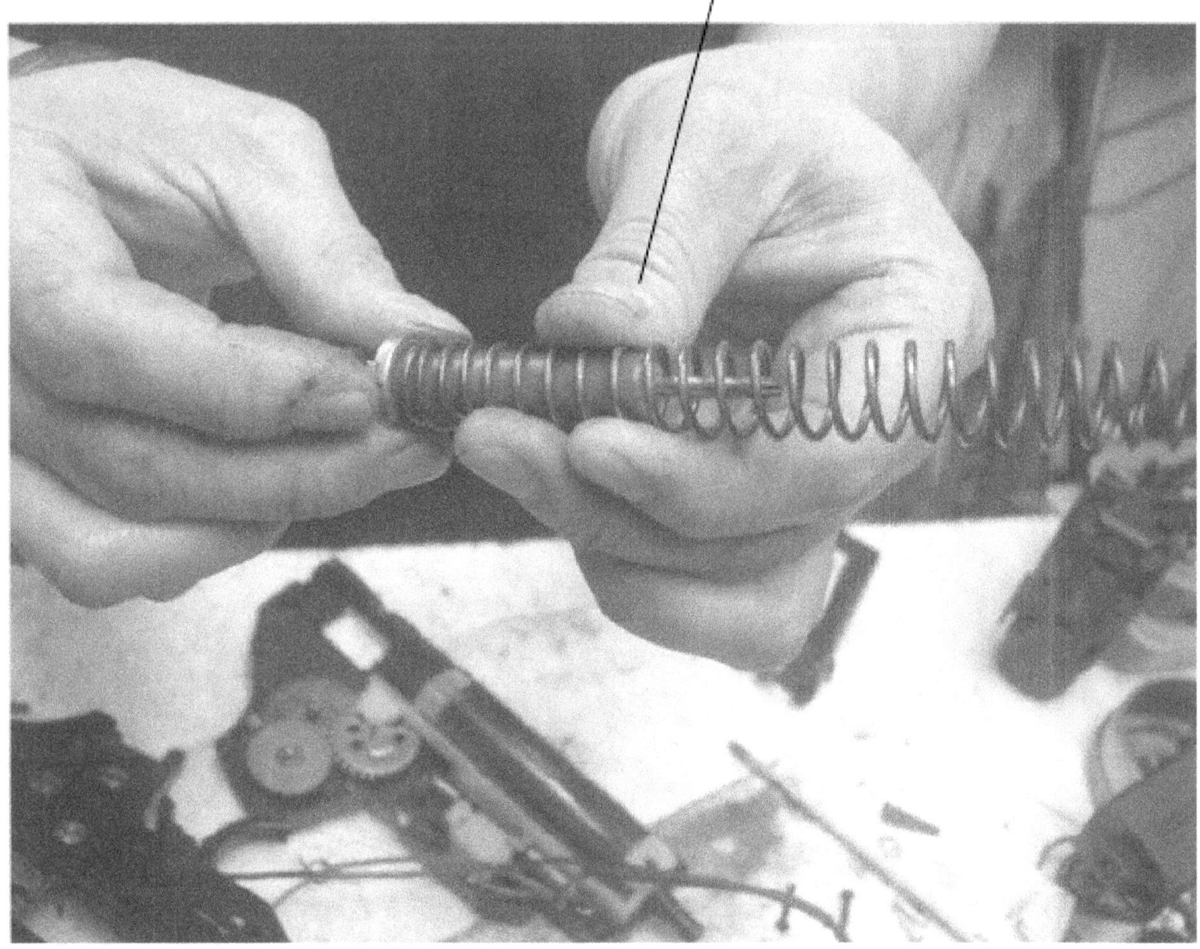

The spring, piston and cylinder set are all contained inside the gearbox. The spring and the spring guide can be easily replaced after opening up the gearbox.

The motor is a standard short motor enclosed in a metal frame. Almost all after-market motors can be used as replacement.

Note the shape of the motor
pinion. Third party products
do not always have a
matching shape. When the
pinion does not match the
bevel gear perfectly, you will
hear a weird sound when the
motor spins.

STRUCTURE OVERVIEW

The KG9 AEG has the following major components:

- The front assembly, which includes the inner barrel, the outer barrel and the front guard (as well as the barrel supporting structure, all in one piece).

- There is a detachable foregrip for housing the battery.

- The body, which includes the lower receiver plus the grip and the butt embedded. There is no separate butt stock.

- The internals, which includes the gearbox and the motor.

- Suppressor is entirely optional.

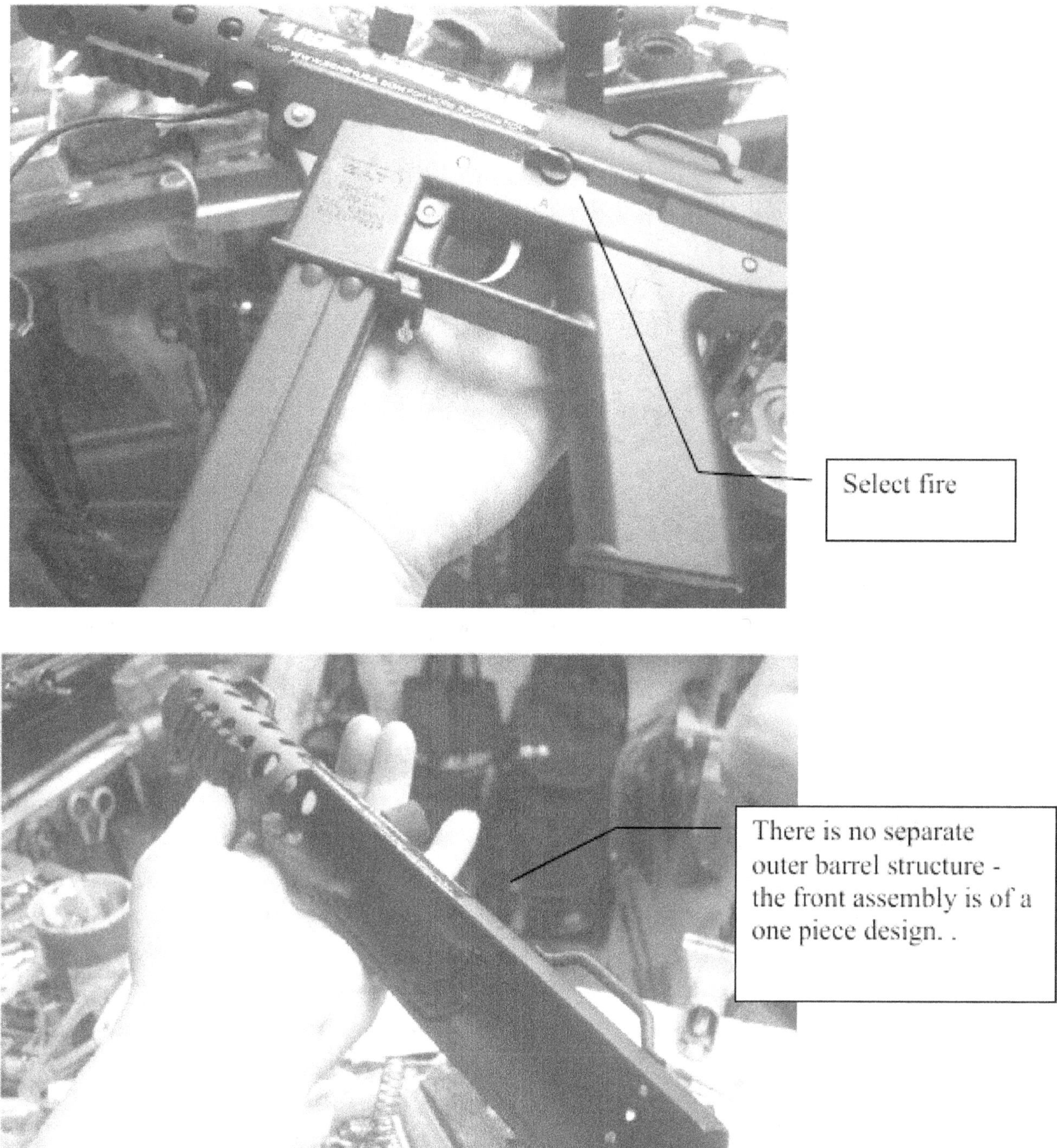
Select fire
There is no separate outer barrel structure - the front assembly is of a one piece design. .

THE FRONT ASSEMBLY AND THE OUTER BARREL

This photo shows the front assembly and the barrel supporting structure.
The select fire switch is on the left hand side of the body. It is mechanical,
just like most other AEG platforms.

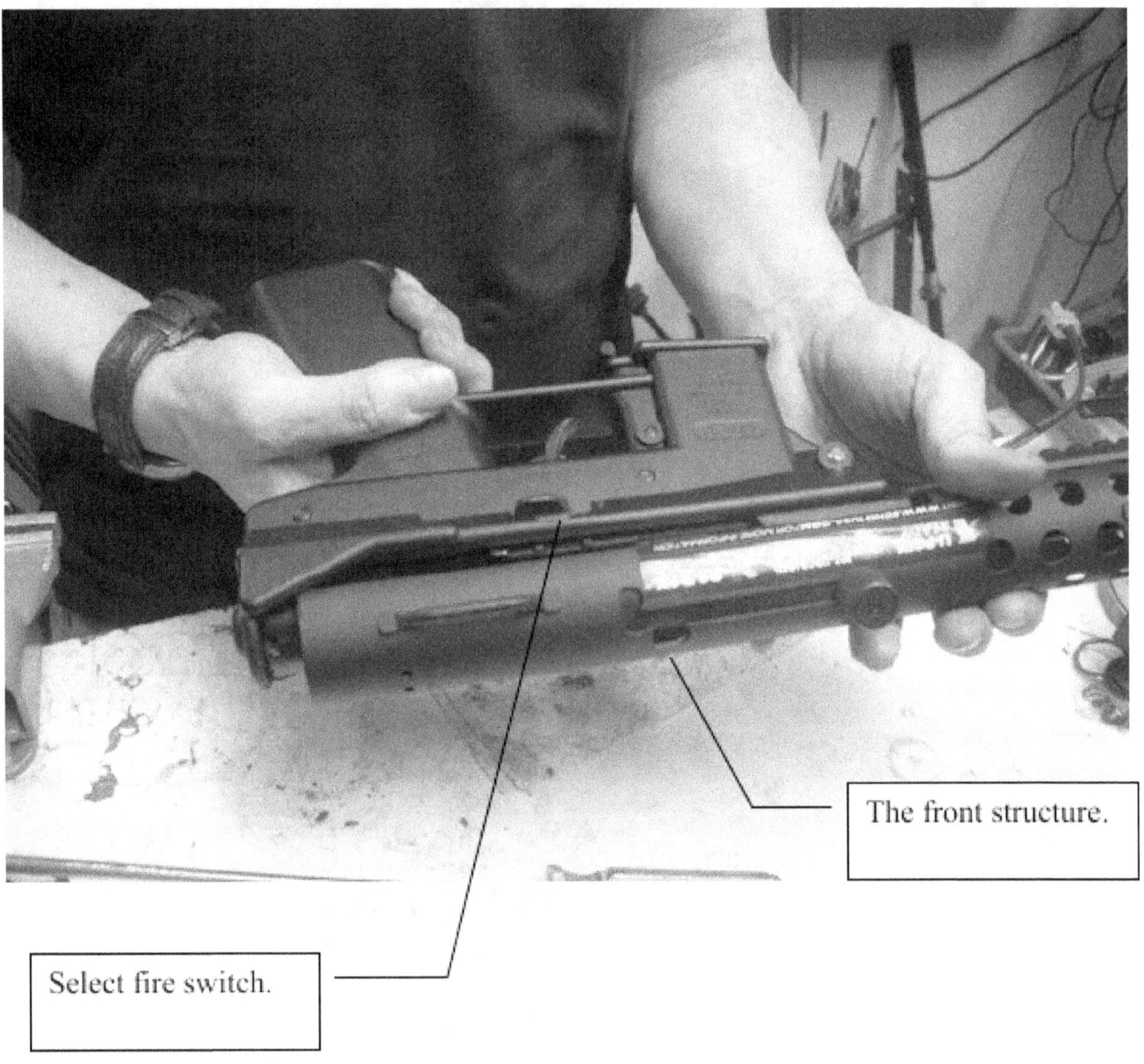

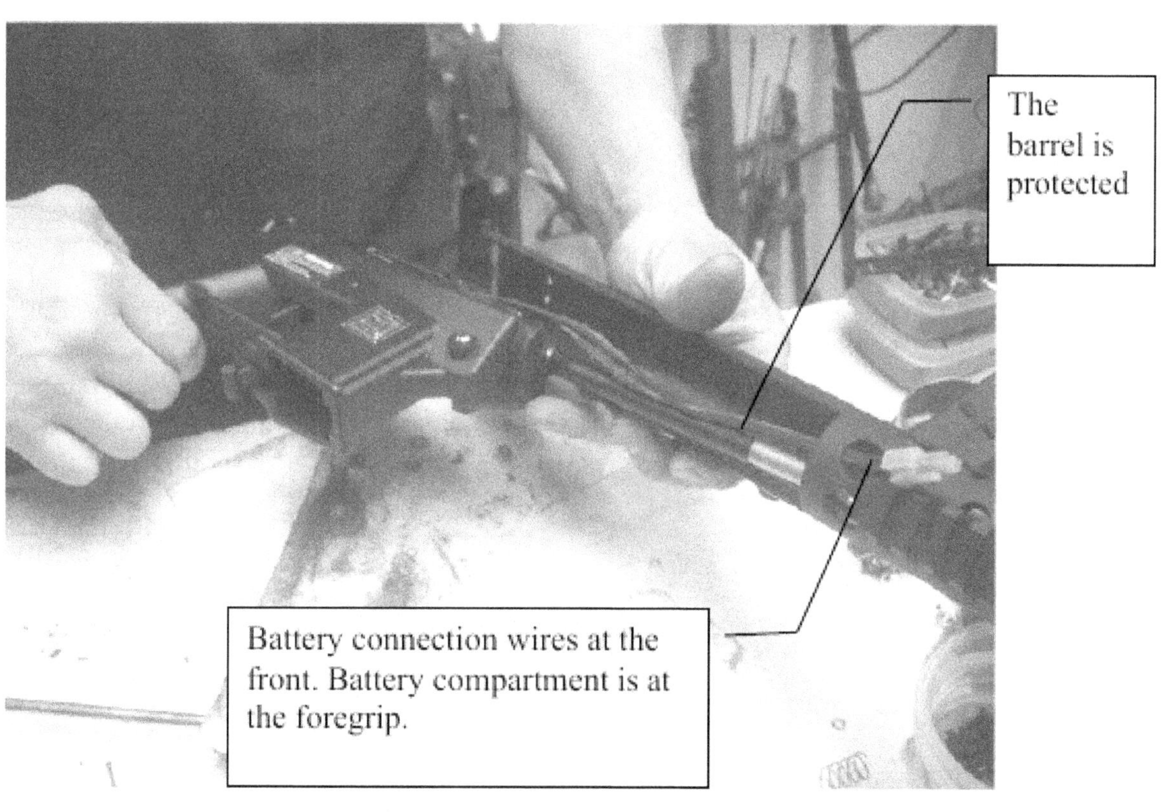

The
barrel is
protected

Battery connection wires at the
front. Battery compartment is at
the foregrip.

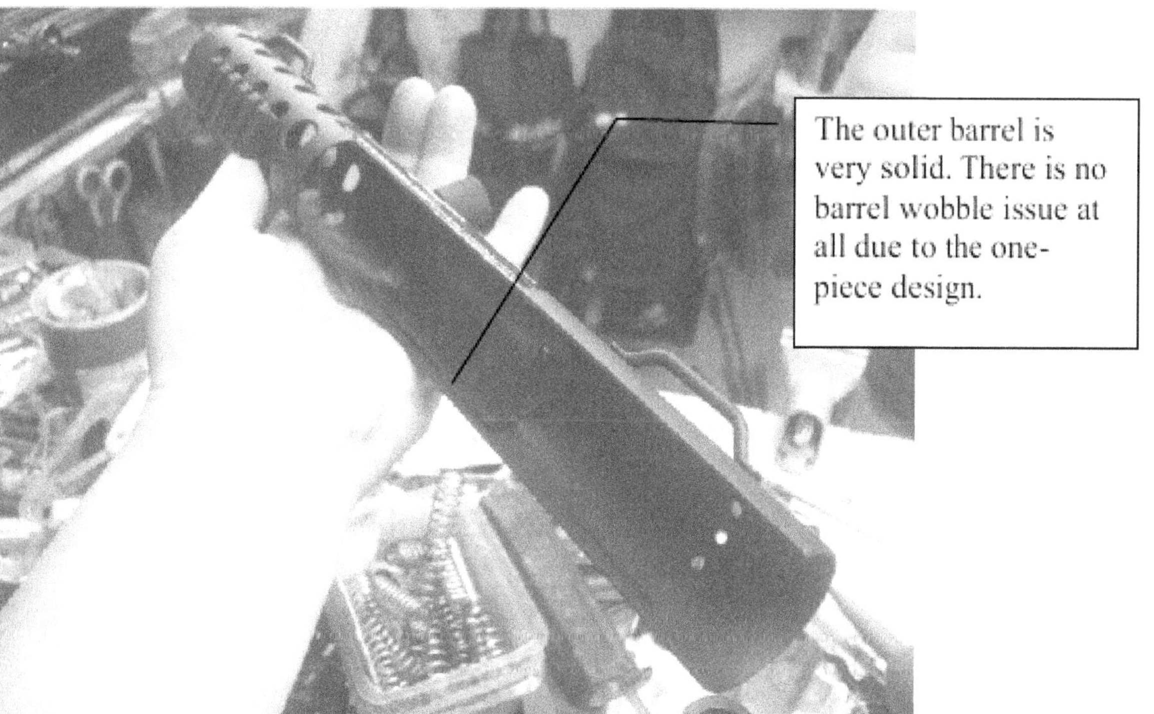

The outer barrel is
very solid. There is no
barrel wobble issue at
all due to the one-
piece design.

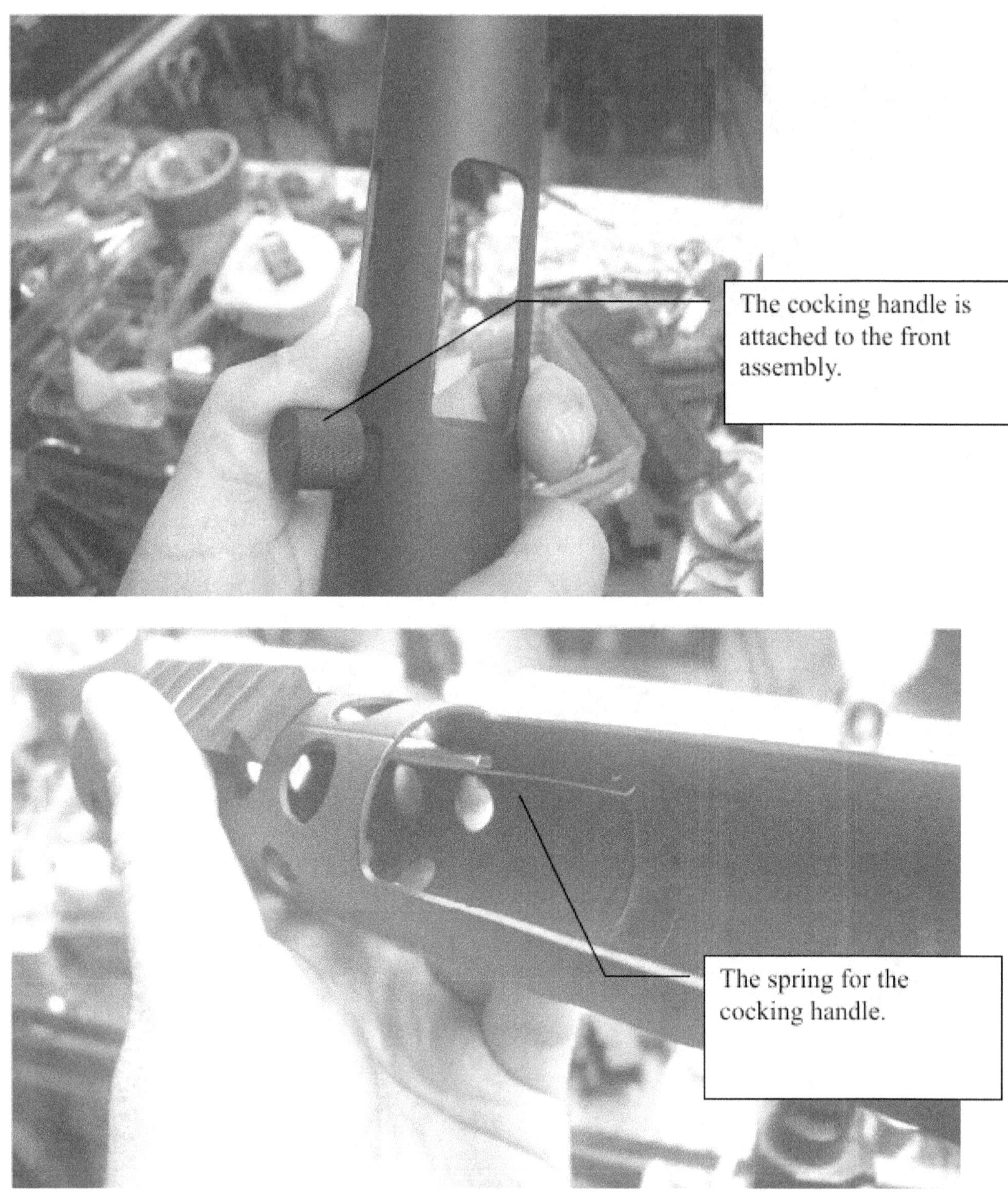

The cocking handle is attached to the front assembly.
The spring for the cocking handle.

THE HOPUP UNIT AND THE INNER BARREL

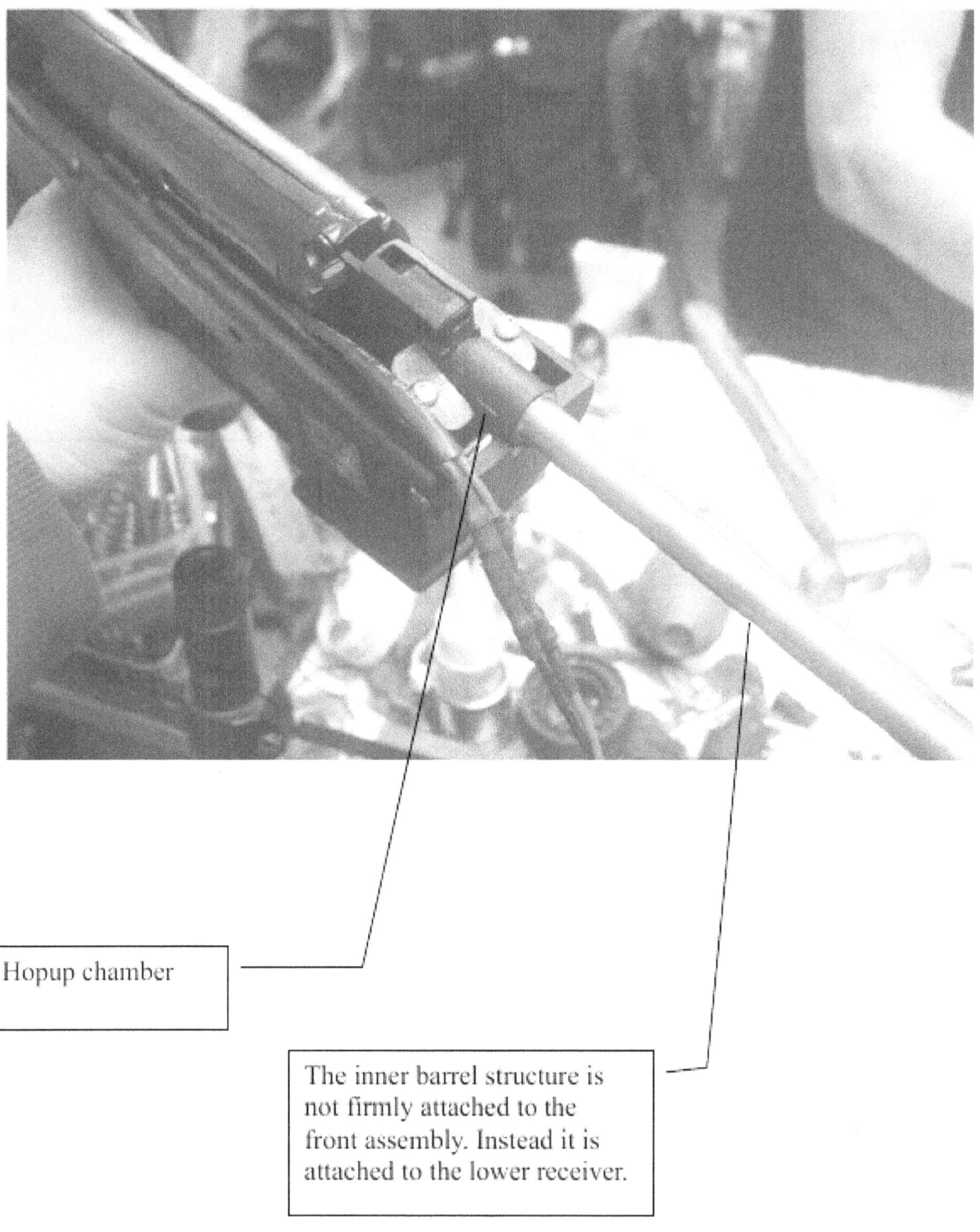

Hopup chamber

The inner barrel structure is not firmly attached to the front assembly. Instead it is attached to the lower receiver.

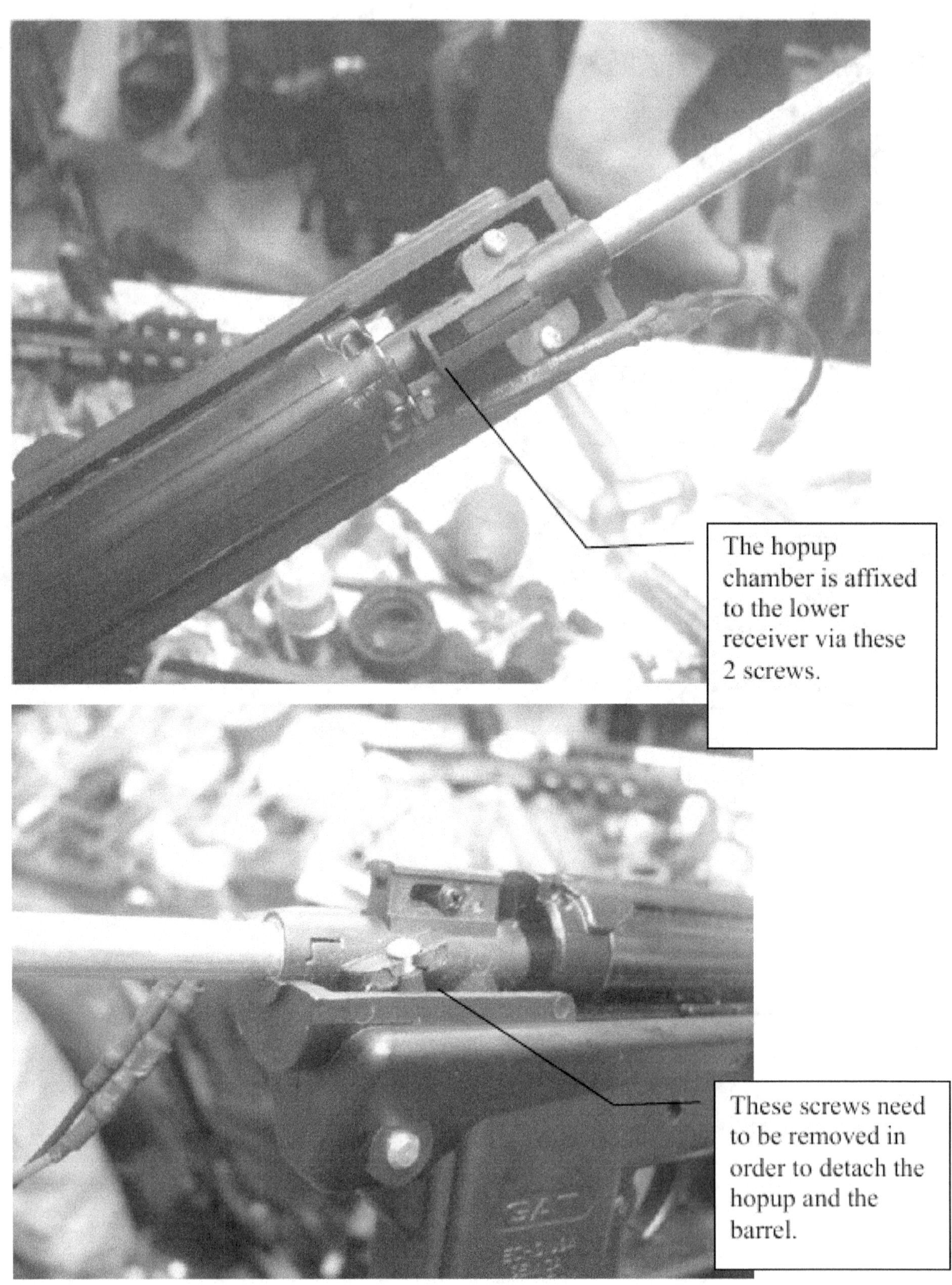

The hopup chamber is affixed to the lower receiver via these 2 screws.

These screws need to be removed in order to detach the hopup and the barrel.

The hopup chamber has a very unique design. It is not third party compatible.

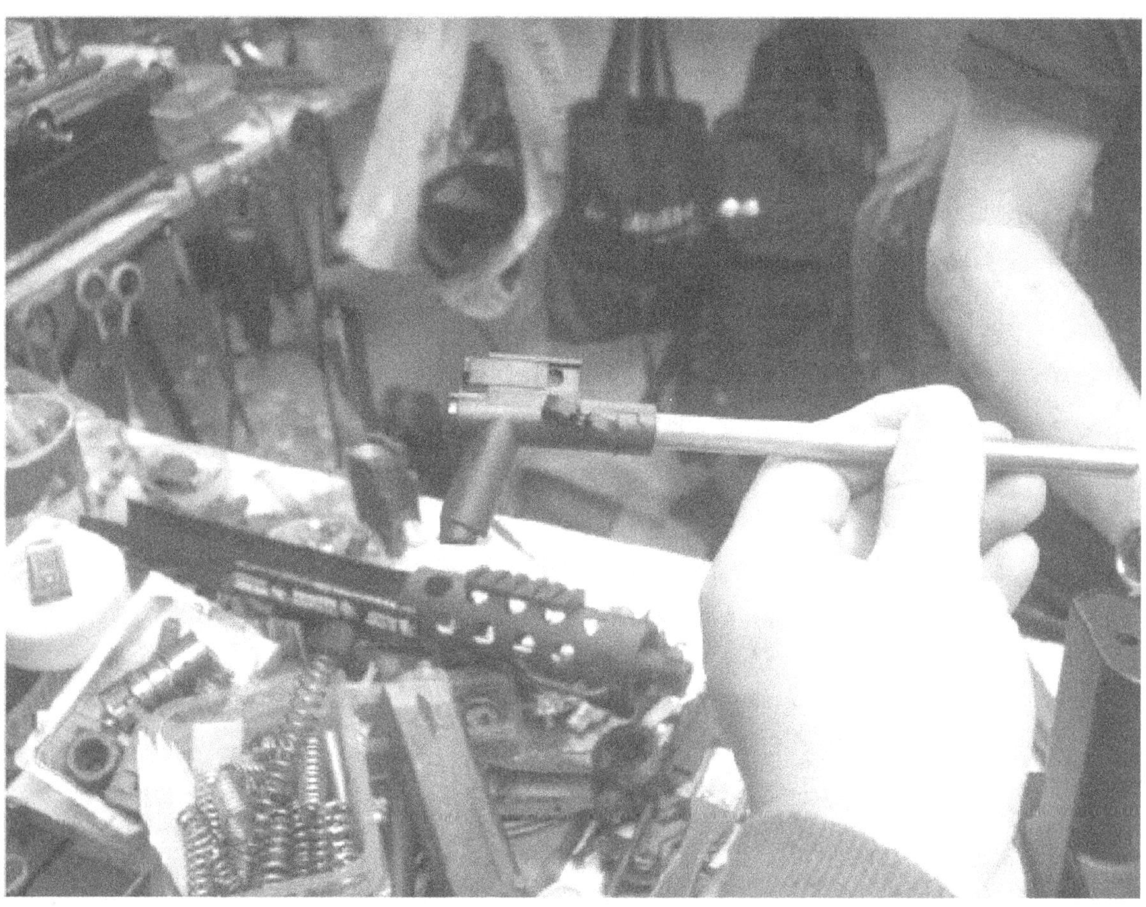

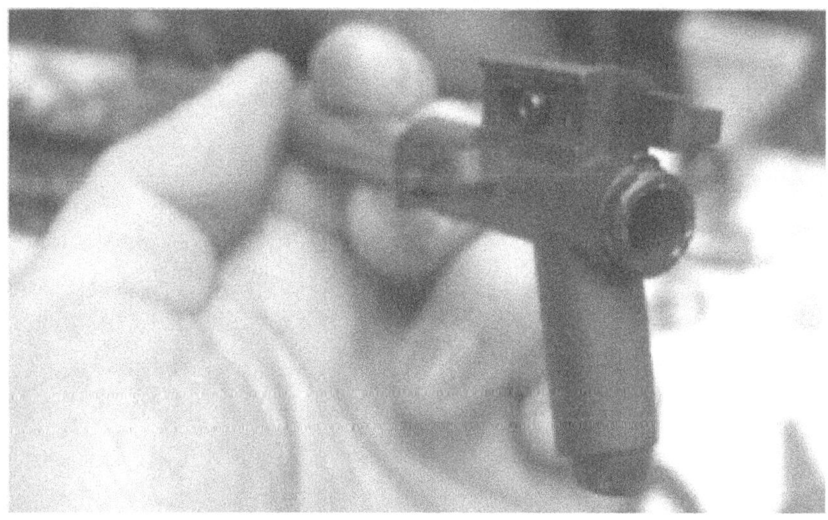

The hopup unit is firmly attached to the inner barrel. It uses an adjustment lever on the side instead of a dial. The chamber is plastic and is composed of several smaller parts. The shape is entirely unique.

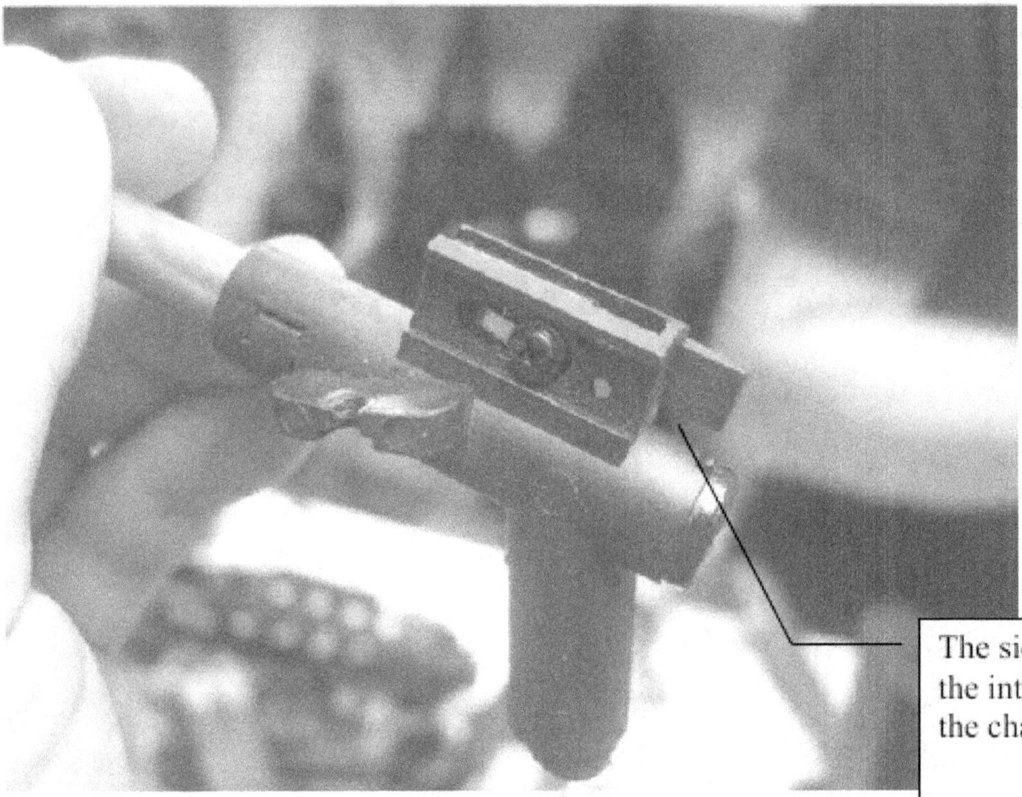

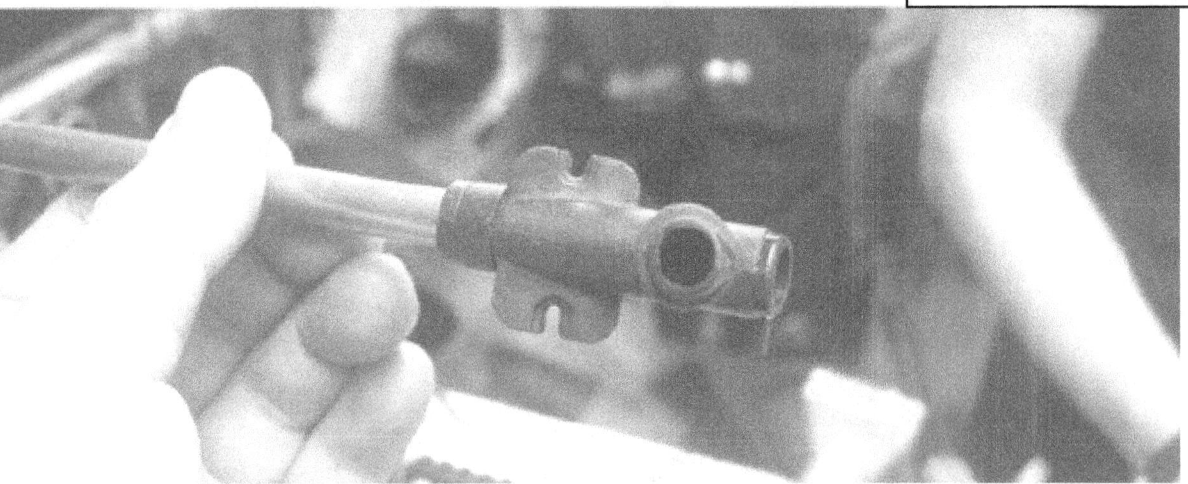

The hopup unit and the inner barrel are two separate components. The inner barrel is "inserted" into the hopup chamber and gets firmly attached accordingly.

The hopup unit produces small friction on the bullet and sets it to back-spin. The amount of friction produced can be adjusted through the rotary dial.

Air leak is often an issue. If the barrel cannot fit tight enough into the hopup chamber, air leak can occur. One quick solution is to use teflon thread seal tape around the inner barrel before inserting it into the hopup chamber.

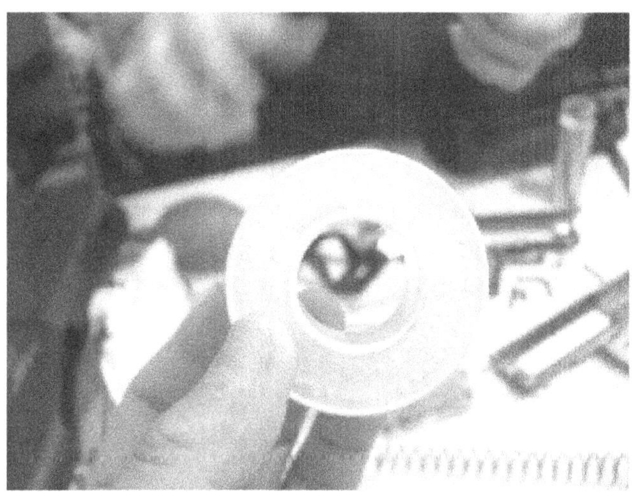

You want to know that the inner barrel determines the size of bullet you can use. All KG9 AEGs use 6mm bullets. In other words, the inner diameter of the barrel is slightly larger than 6mm (somewhere between 6.03mm and 6.09mm).

A barrel that is too tight can be problematic. You need to realize that not all bullets are perfectly 6mm. Some are slightly larger due to inaccuracy in the manufacturing process. These bullets can easily jam the barrel. On the other hand, if the barrel is too large, there is room for air to leak out, thus leading to poor performance and wasted power.

Barrel length is related to accuracy. Generally speaking, the longer the barrel the more accurate the gun would shoot. Do realize that a long outer barrel would not help. To increase accuracy you need a longer inner barrel. Also, when you increase the inner barrel length you will also need to change the configuration of your gearbox, which is beyond the scope of this book.

The KG9 inner barrel is quite short (but not as short as that of a MP5K). If you want to install a longer barrel, make sure you have it properly protected by a mock suppressor.

THE LOWER GUN BODY

As can be seen from the photo below, there is an upper gun body and a lower gun body. You can slide open the body and expose the gearbox. To open up the body, the first thing to do is to remove the rear sight.

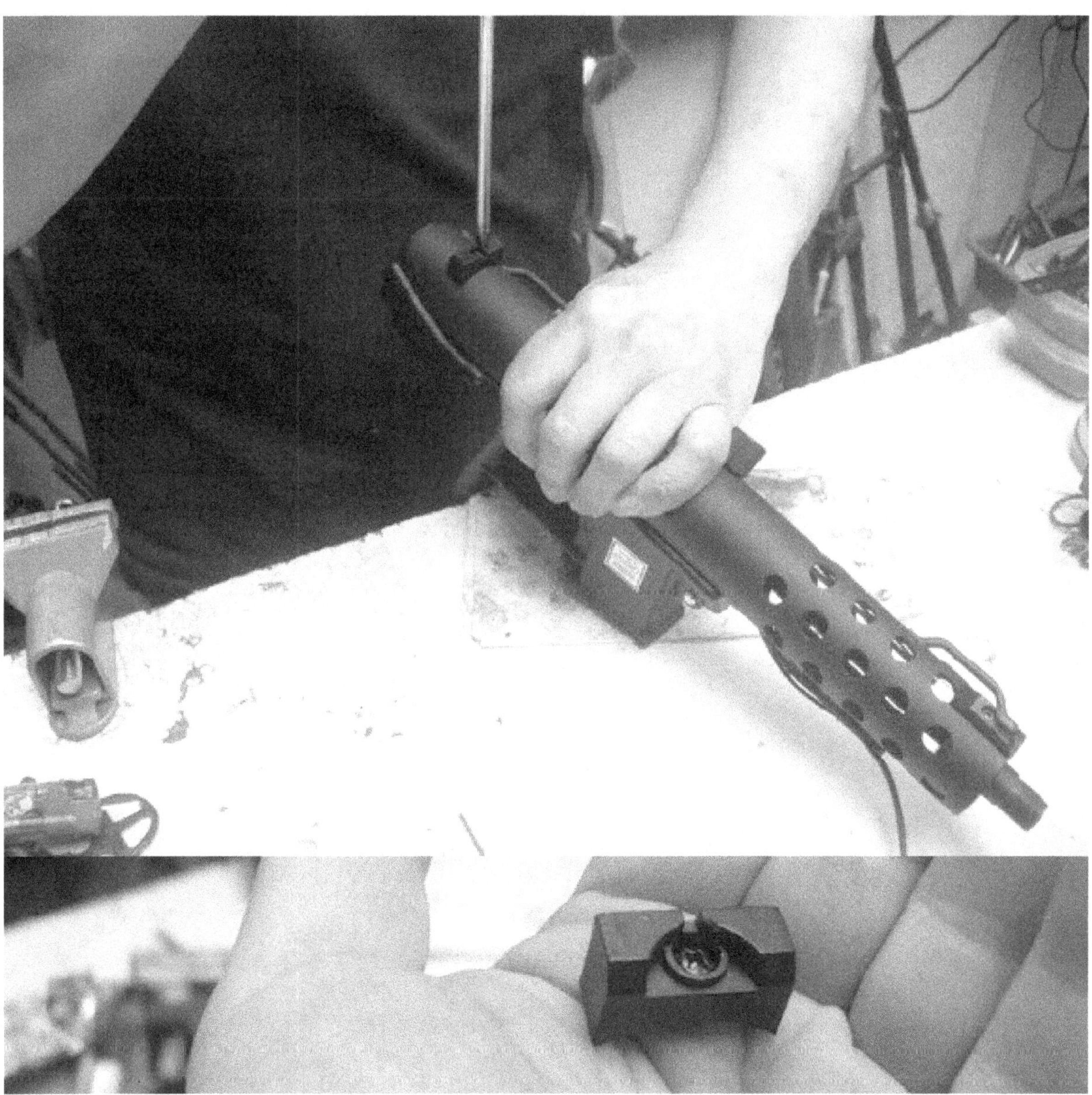

      AirsoftPRESS (Hong Kong). All rights reserved.

The gearbox is still sitting on the lower receiver. You need to knock off a pin from the receiver and remove a hex screw from the butt. You also need to detach the hopup unit before you can take out the gearbox.

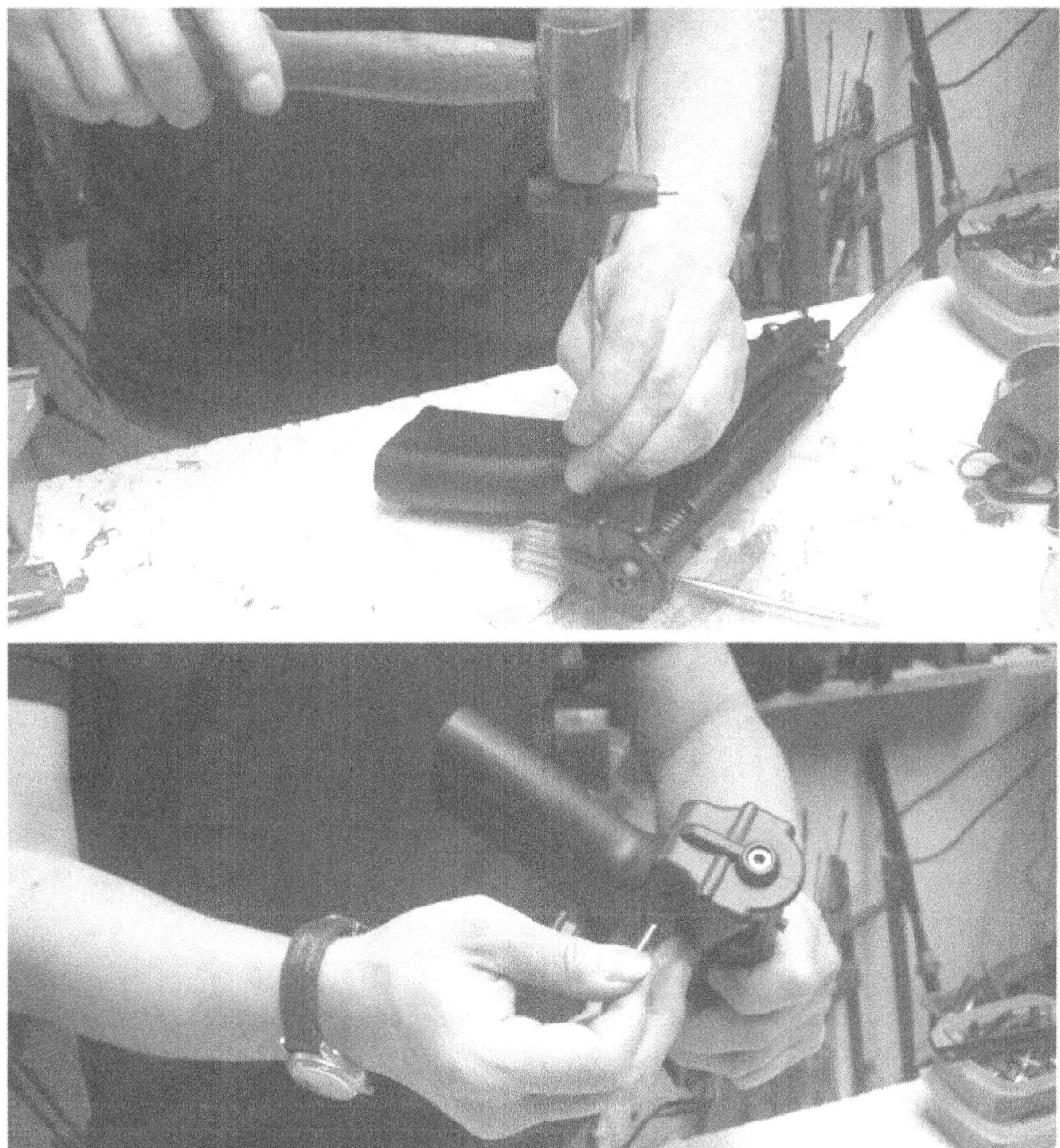

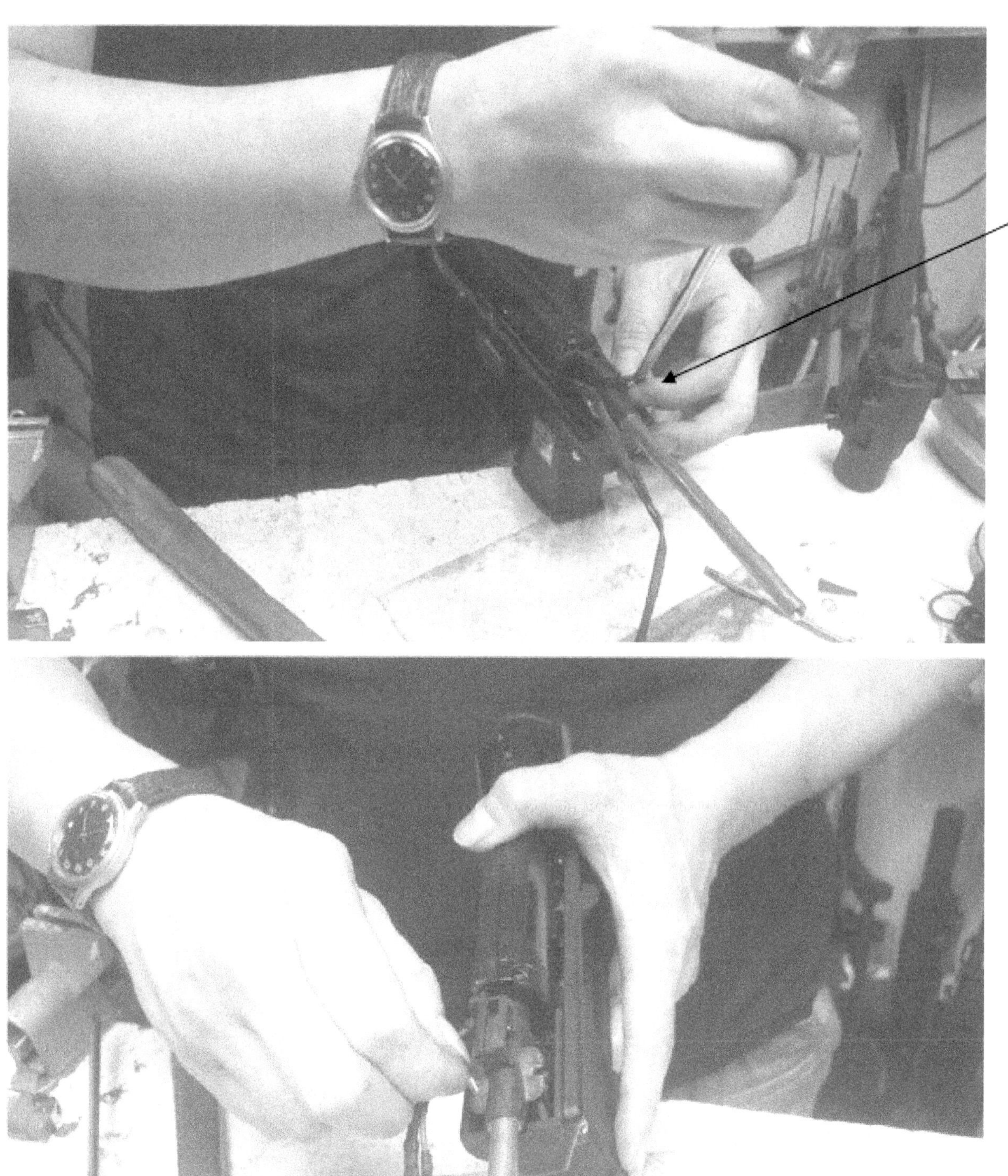

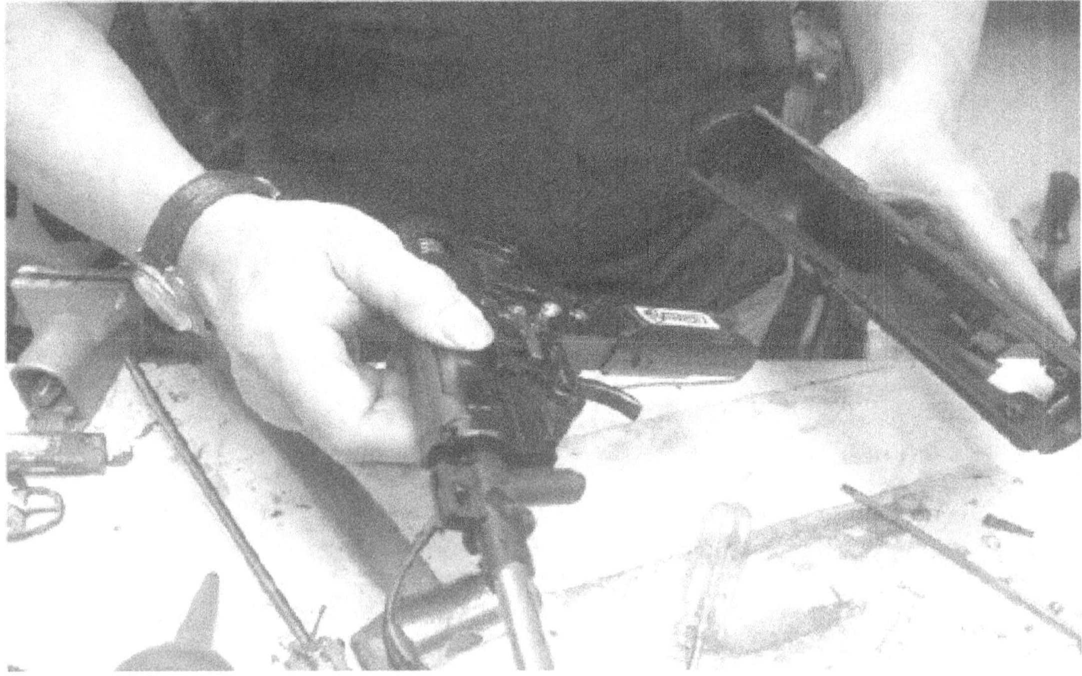

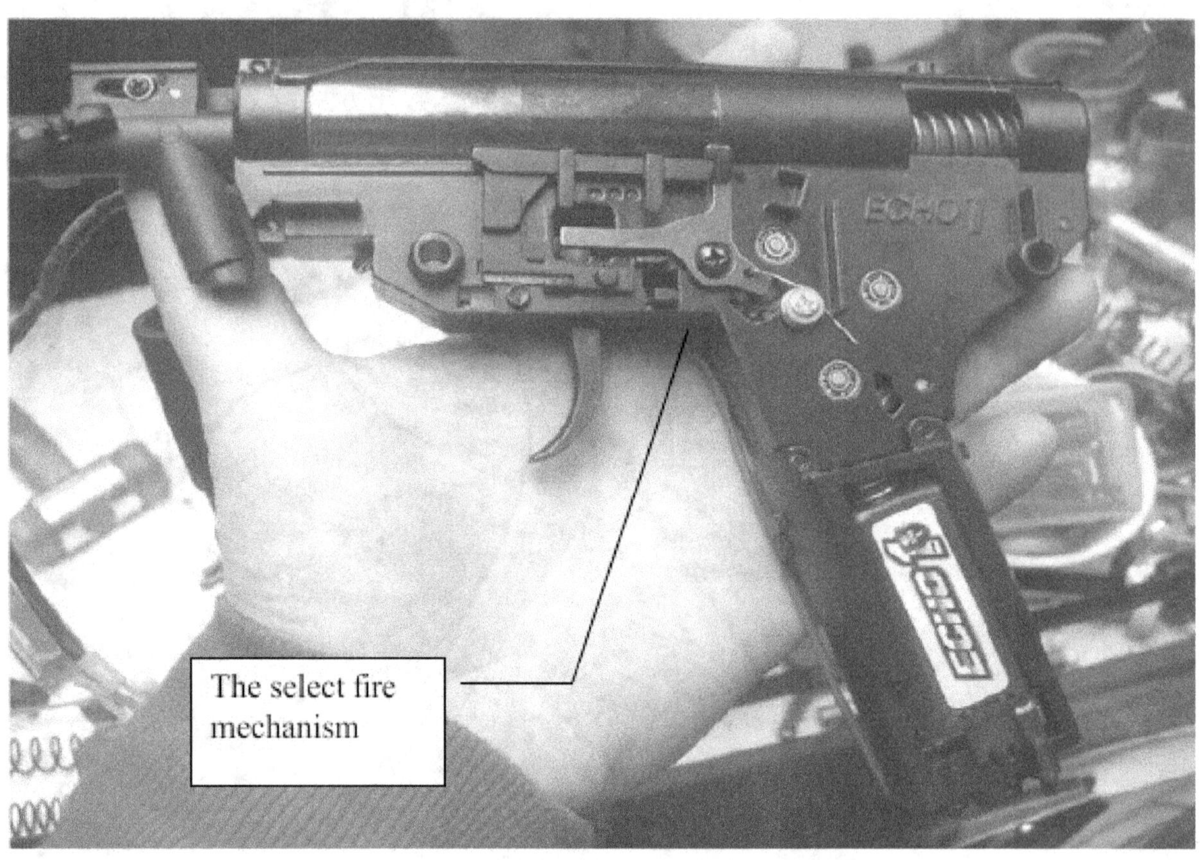

The motor resides in the mounting frame, which is inside the pistol grip (which is part of the lower receiver structure). Adjustment can be made from the bottom via a small hex screw.

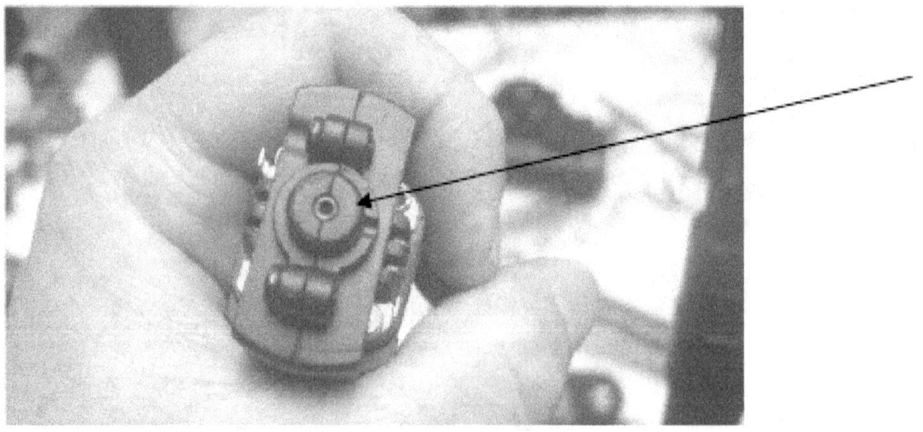

This is how the motor can be taken out from the enclosure.

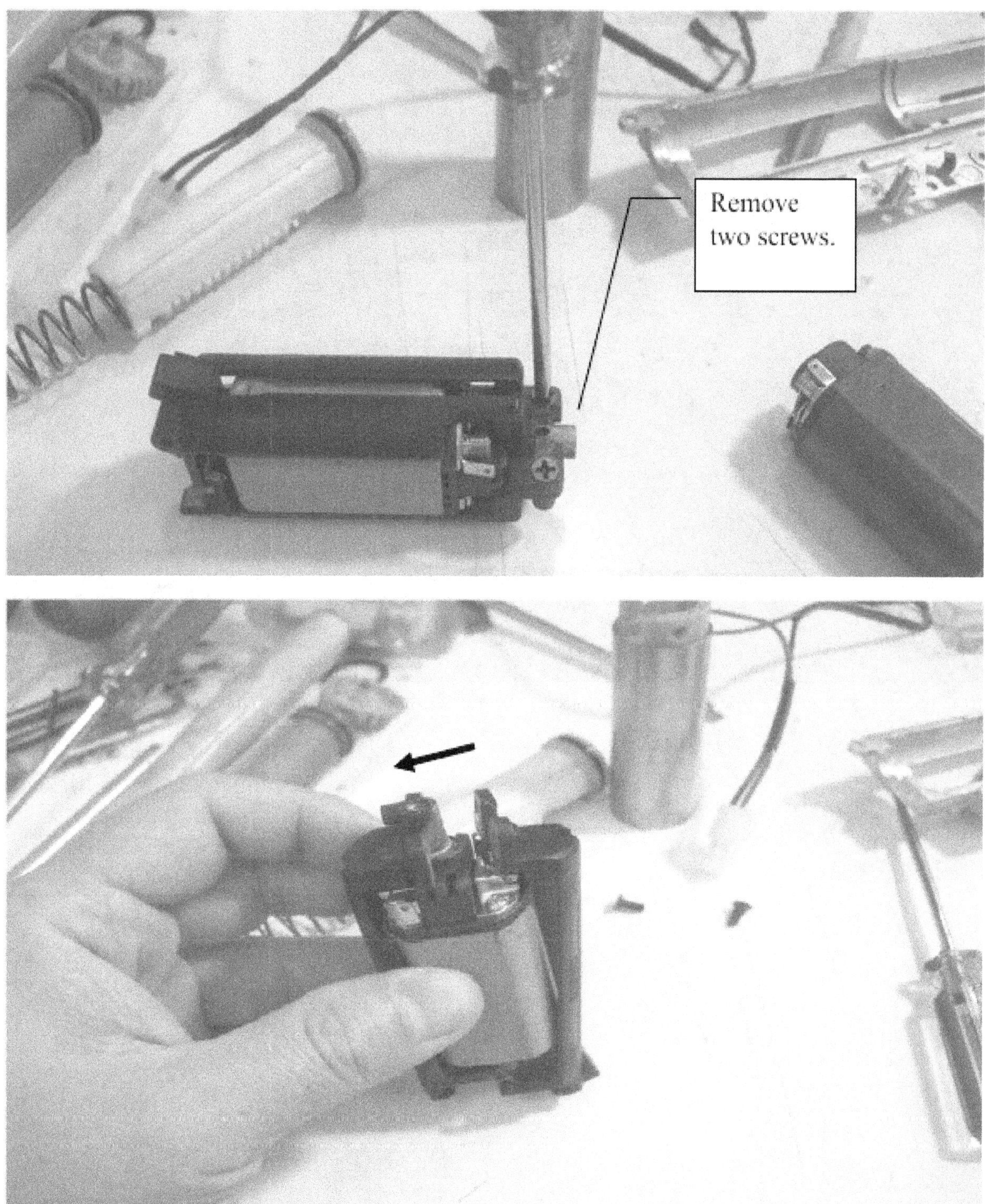

This little plate is for motor positioning adjustment. Make sure it is properly placed.

You want to check the motor brushes. If the brushes are seriously worn out, replace them. In a high power configuration they tend to get worn out real fast.

Motor brush is a consumable item.

SUMMARY OF THE STRUCTURE AND THE MAJOR COMPONENTS

As a summary:

- The inner barrel is protected by the front assembly (which includes the upper body and the outer barrel in a one-piece structure).

- The hopup unit is firmly attached to the inner barrel. This unit is NOT third party compatible. Therefore, unless strictly necessary you should not attempt to play with it…

- The foregrip is detachable and is for hosting the battery.

- The gearbox sits on the lower receiver. The trigger unit follows the gearbox.

- The pistol grip is part of the lower receiver structure. You cannot take it out or detach it.

- There is no separate butt stock.

- The mags are unique.

EXAMINING THE GEARBOX

The KG9 gearbox uses internals that are mostly compatible with third party offerings. The gearbox shell is unique though.

The first thing you should do to open the gearbox is to detach the motor mounting frame (2 screws here). Then you remove the remaining gearbox hex screws one by one.

You need to be very careful with these hex screws. Hex screws are always subject to fairly easy stripping.

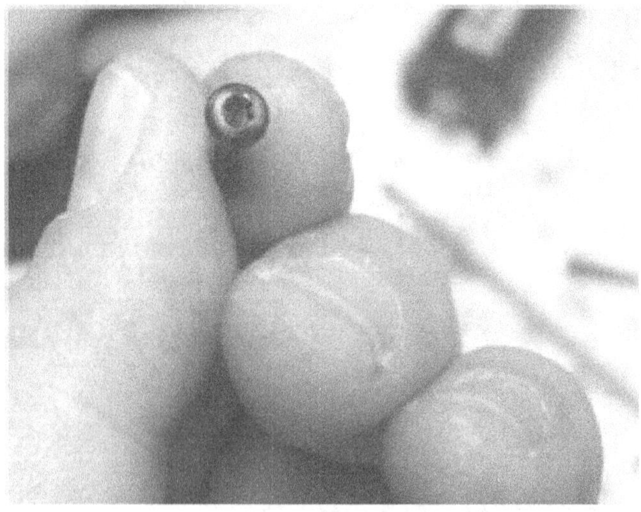

Now you are ready to open up the shell.

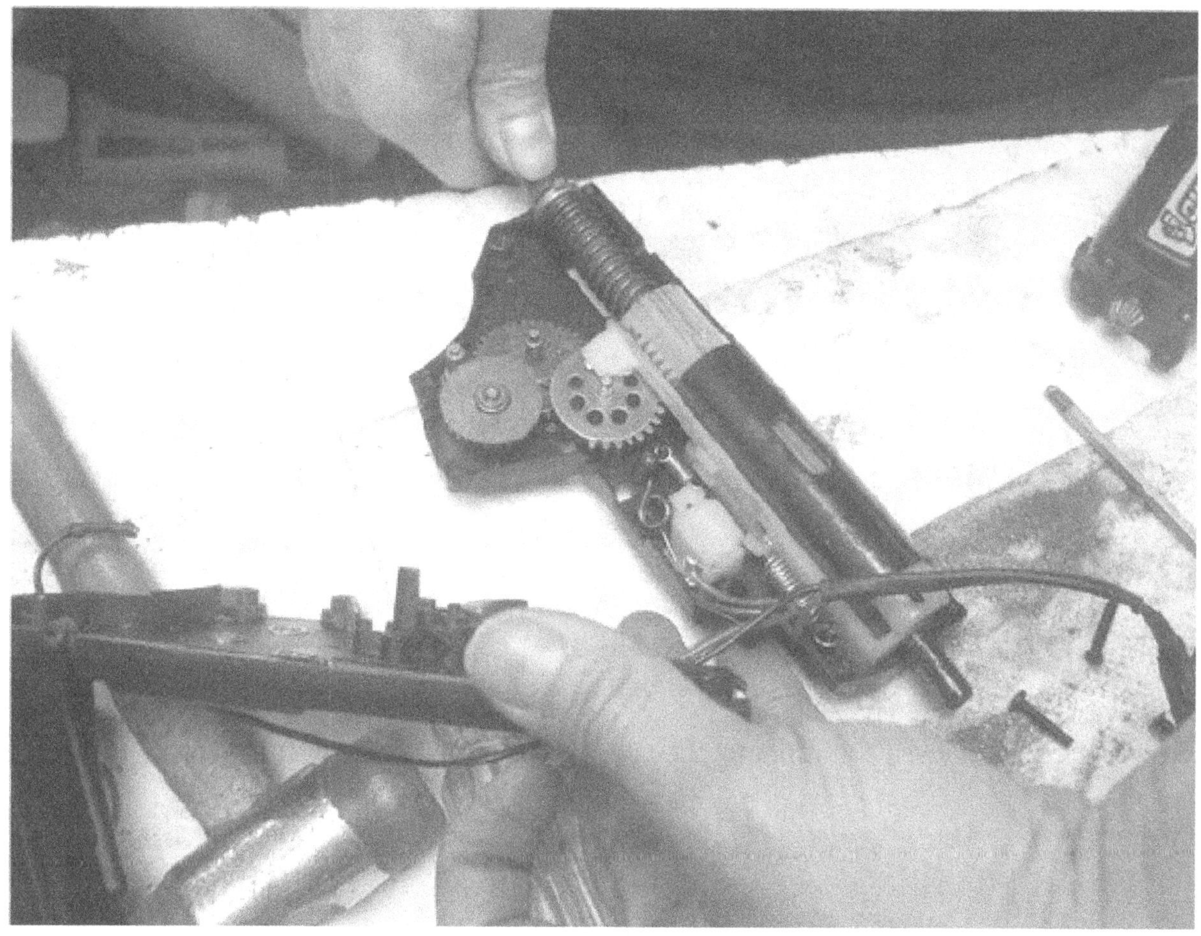

A high quality shell is stiff (so it can withstand high impact), with highly accurate measurement. High quality bushings or bearings can facilitate the smooth rotation of gears. Typical size of ball bearings for upgraded gearbox is 8mm. There are a total of 6 bearings, with 3 on each side. Replacing the stock ones with 9mm ball bearings / bushings is possible if you know how to enlarge the place holders properly.

Generally speaking, ball bearings can allow for smoother rotation with less friction. However, structurally they are weaker than metal bushings.

Be very careful with the spring. It can fly out and get you hurt!

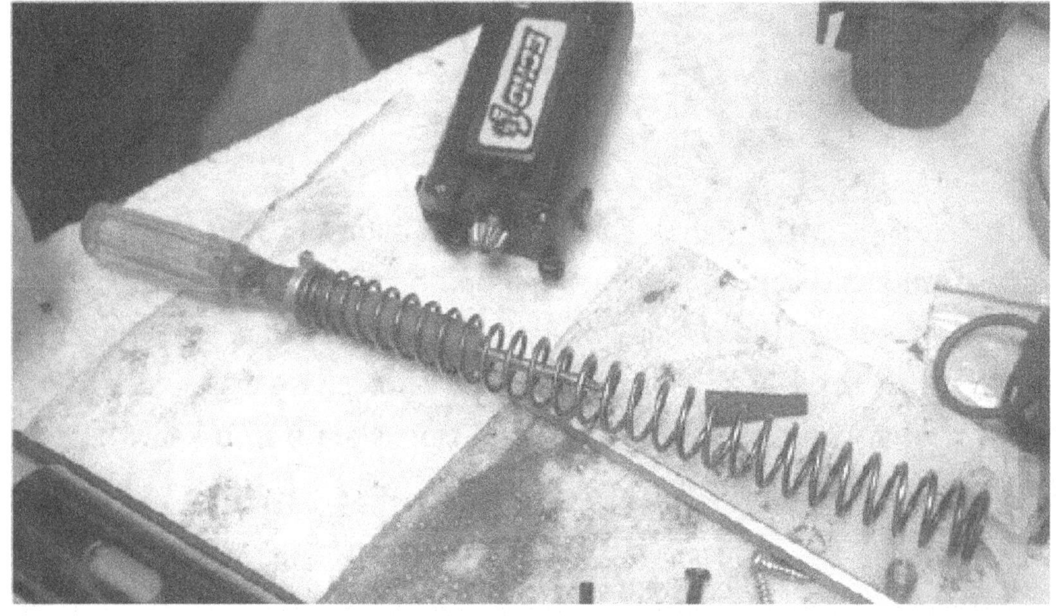

You should slowly take out the spring and then slide out the piston. You do this to free the gears.

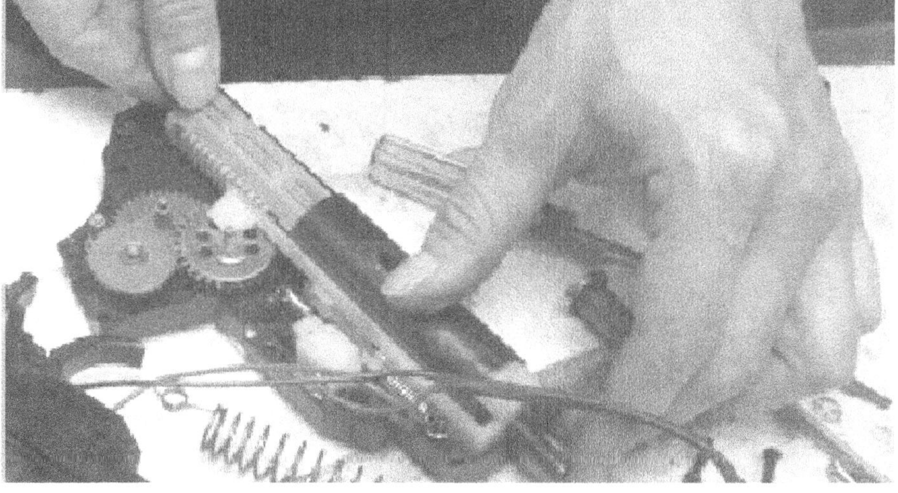

Anti
reversal
Spur gear
The motor drives this
bevel gear.
Sector gear
Built-in delayer

It is the sector gear that drives the piston. The anti-reversal interacts with
the bevel gear.

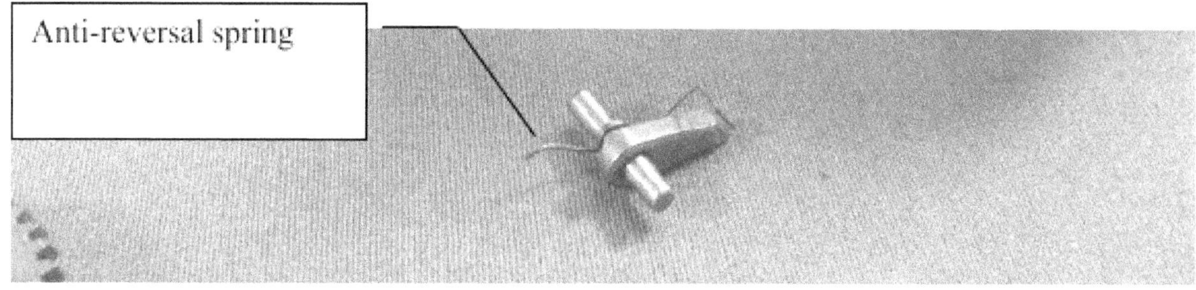

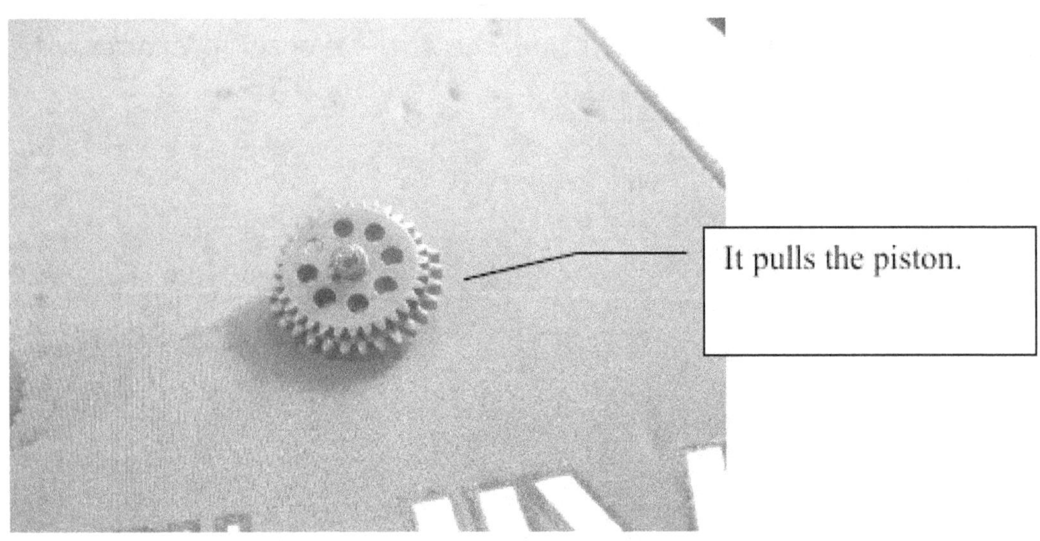

The sector gear and the spur gear.

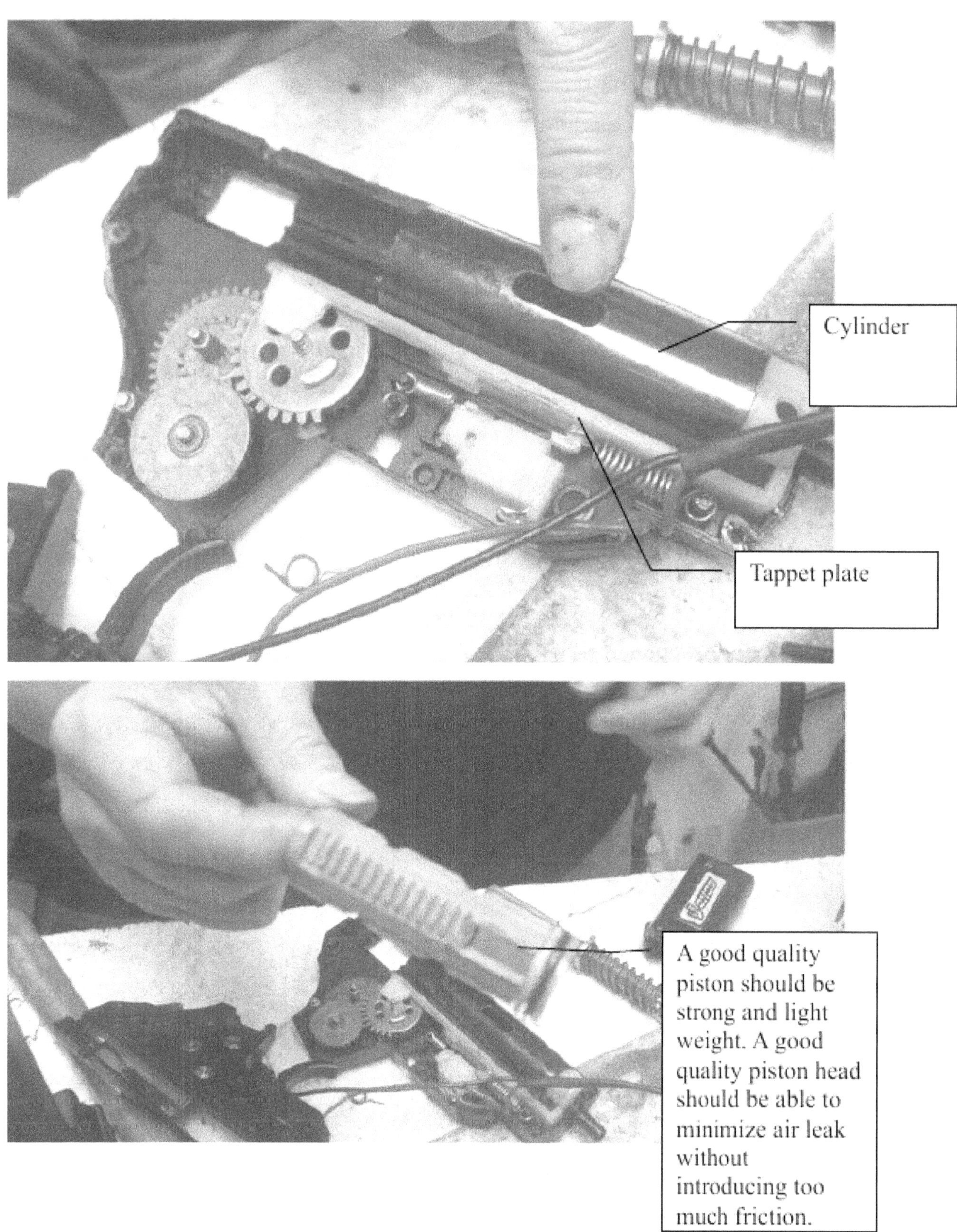

Cylinder
Tappet plate
A good quality
piston should be
strong and light
weight. A good
quality piston head
should be able to
minimize air leak
without
introducing too
much friction.

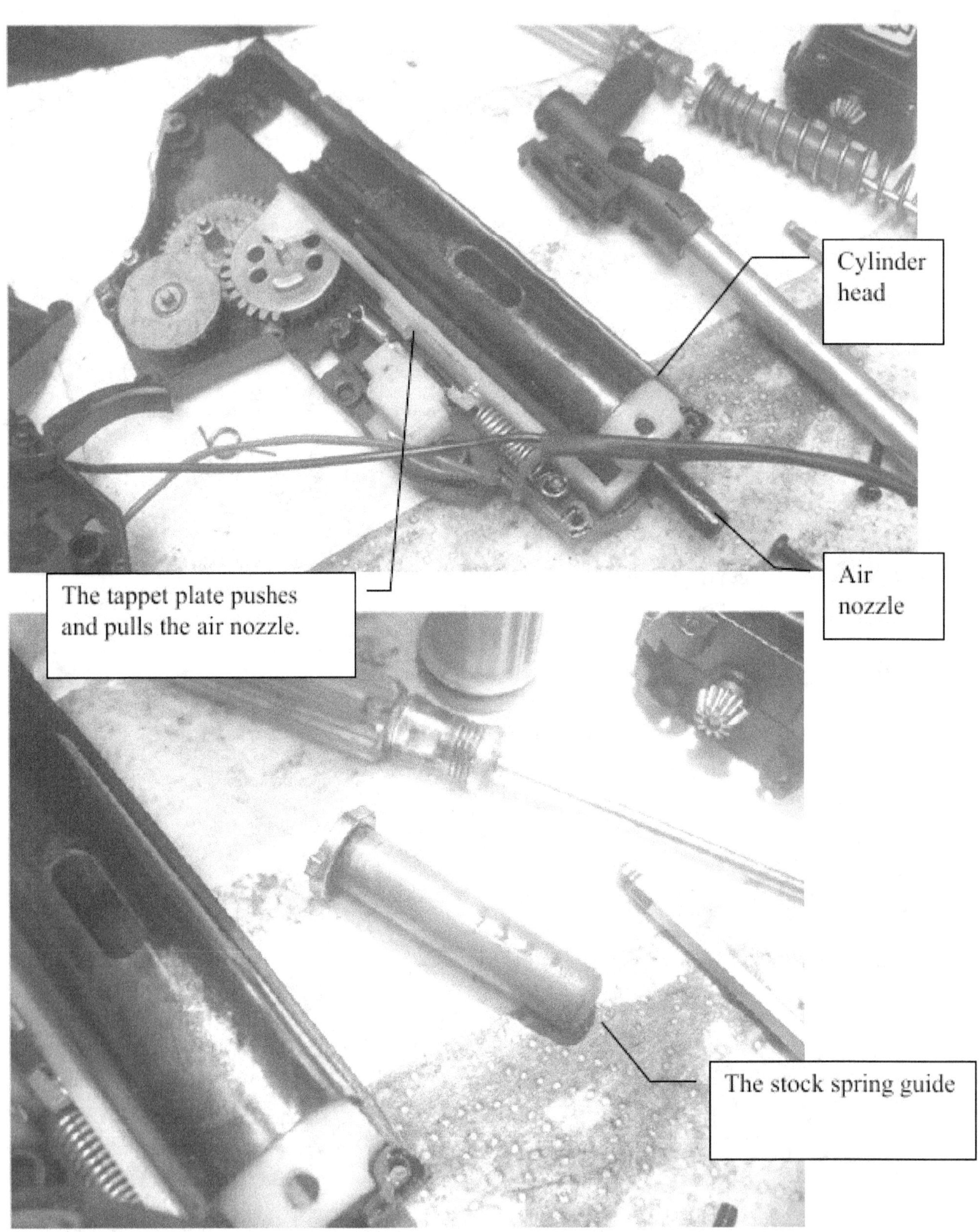

Cylinder
head

Air
nozzle

The tappet plate pushes
and pulls the air nozzle.

The stock spring guide

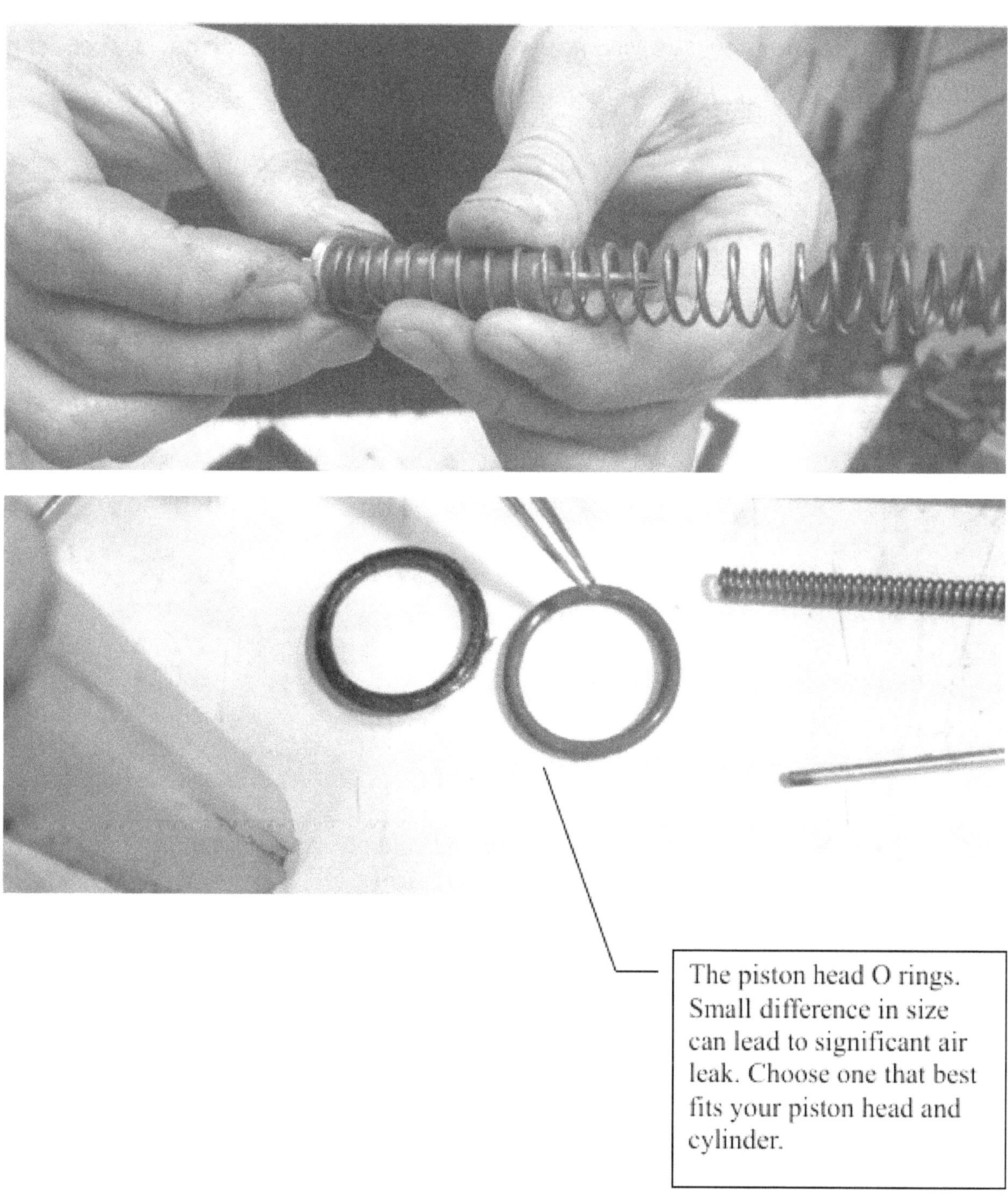

The piston head O rings. Small difference in size can lead to significant air leak. Choose one that best fits your piston head and cylinder.

Generally, the thicker the spring wire the stiffer the spring is. You can compare different springs by measuring their wire thickness.

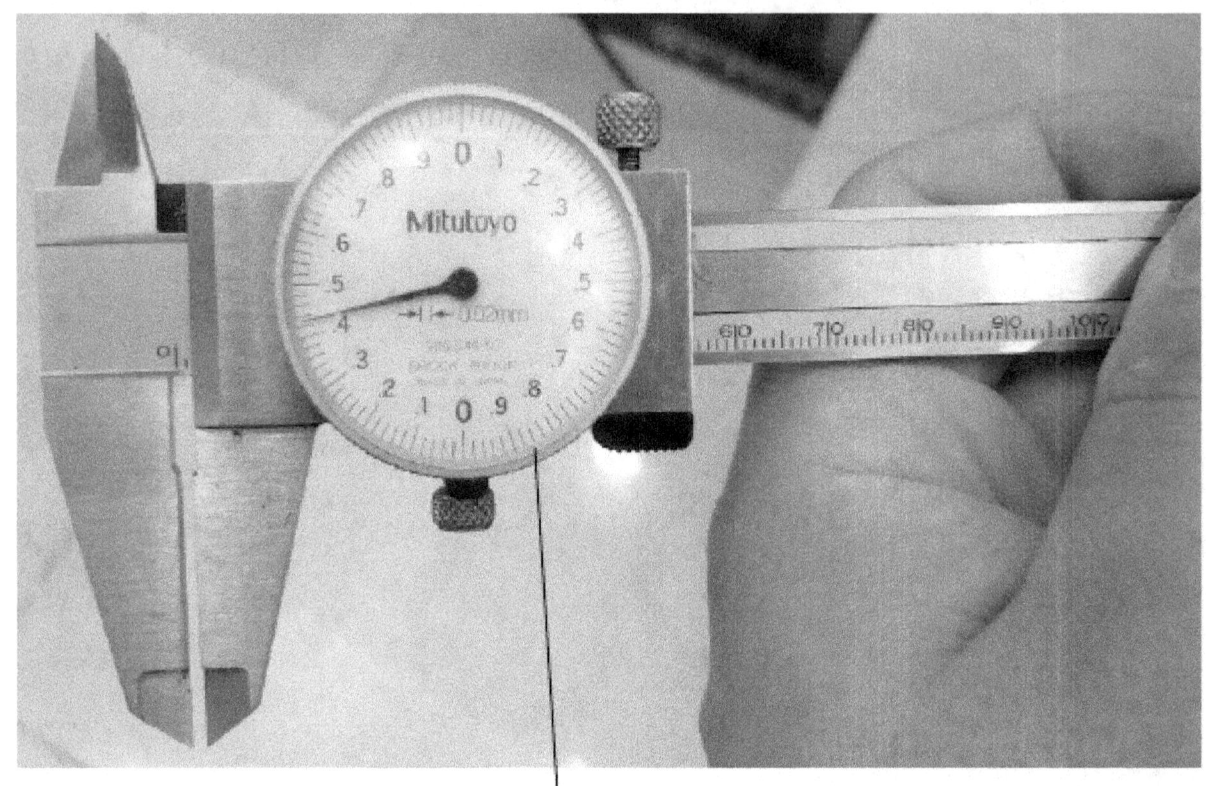

Hand held precision measuring instrument

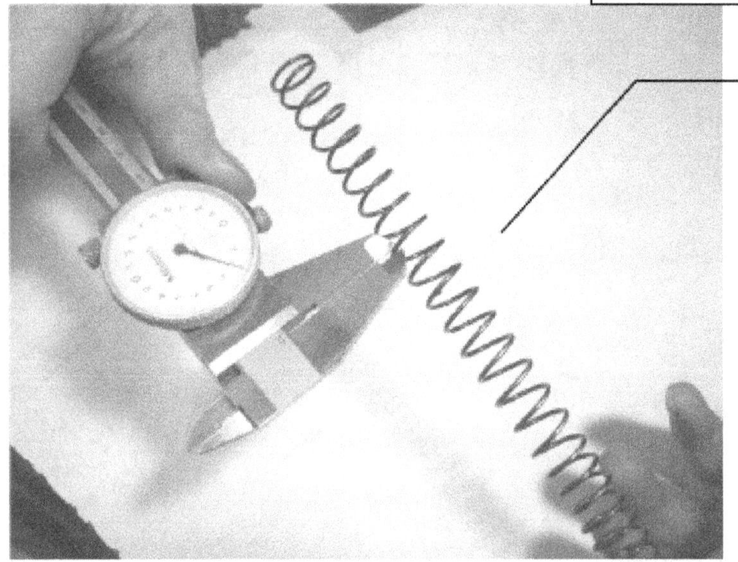

Another factor is the length and the number of coils. Longer spring with more coils tend to be "more powerful".

Some springs go with the M rating. For example, a M120 spring may mean "120MPS power". Do note that this rating is manufacturer assigned and may not always be accurate.

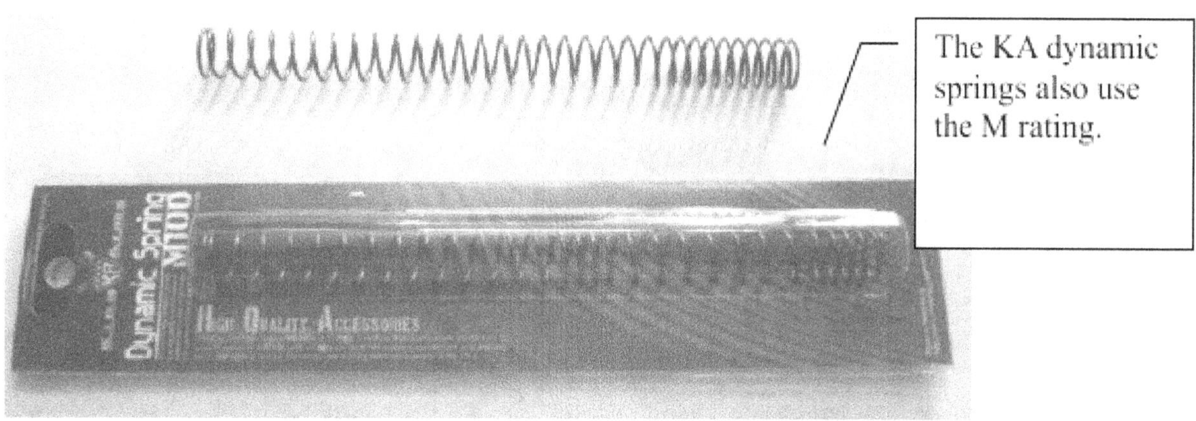

The KA dynamic springs also use the M rating.

The spring has to push the piston. A heavy piston is supposed to be able to produce higher impact force. HOWEVER, since it is heavier it will travel slower. The reduction in speed may offset the performance gain.

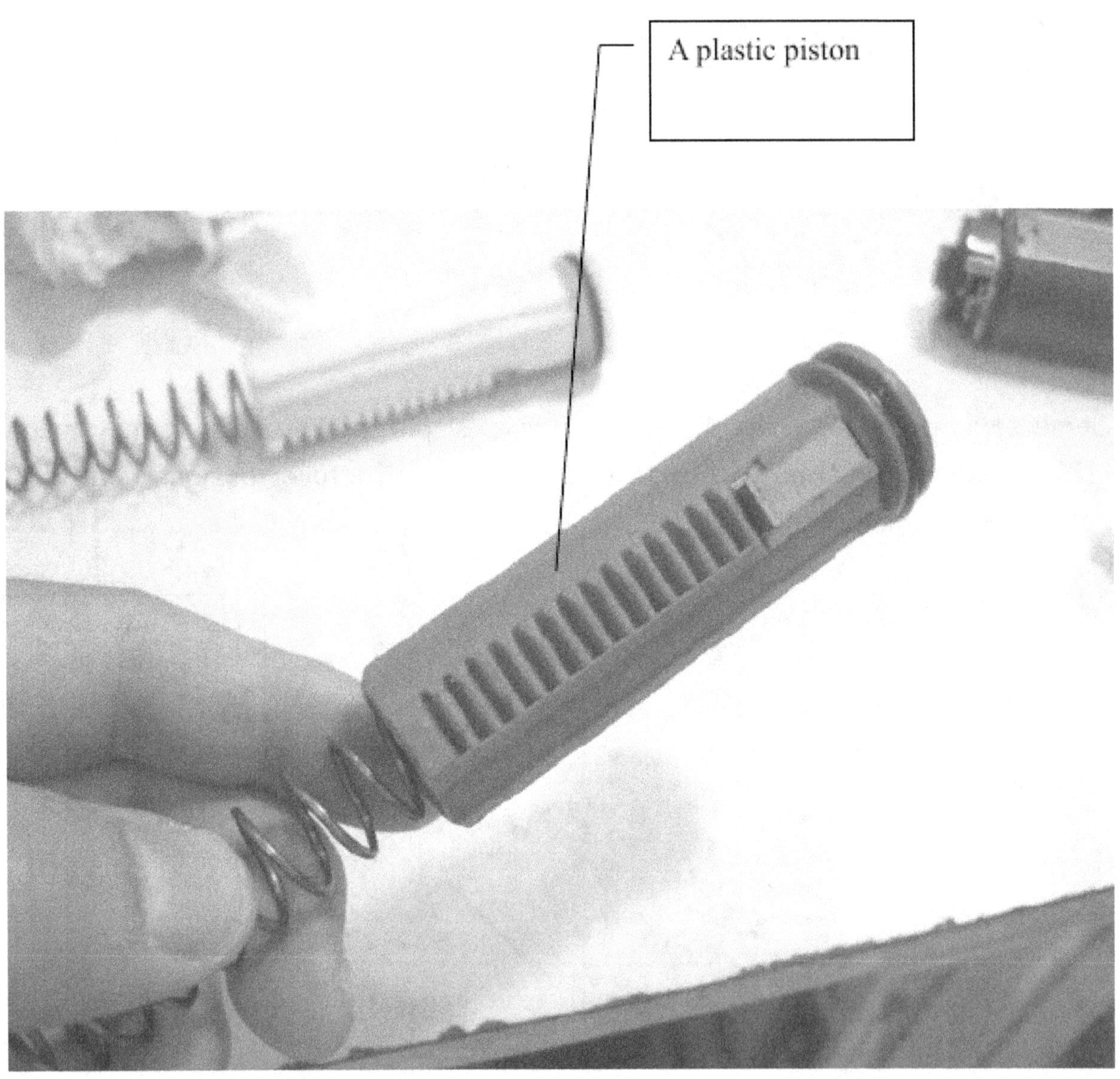

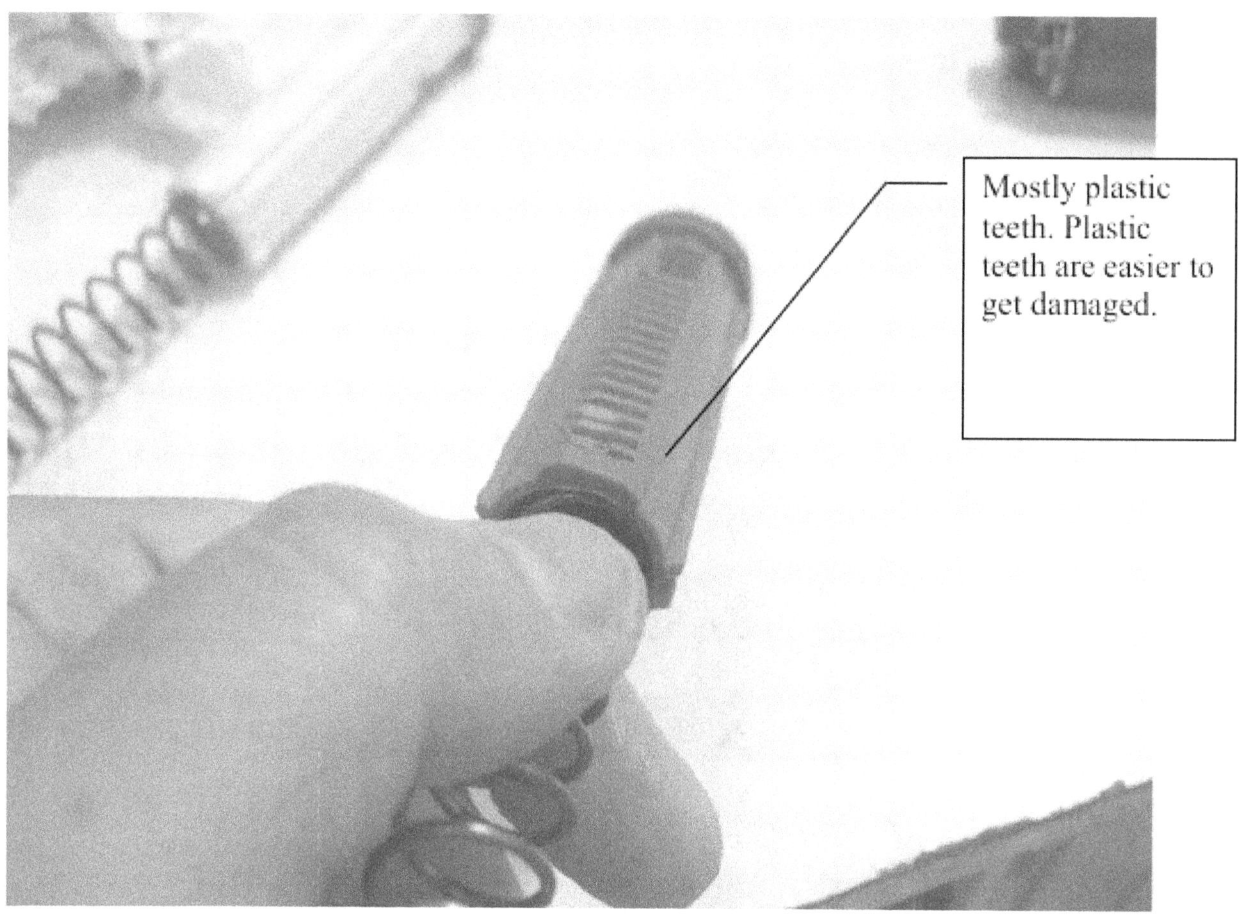

Using light weight material for the piston at the expense of strength is not preferable. With a stiff spring the impact force produced can be huge. Therefore, you need a piston that can survive the impact force.

Piston with plastic teeth does have the advantage of ease of modification (say, teeth removal). Teeth removal is pretty common these days … people like to remove one tooth from the piston to avoid unnecessary scratching...

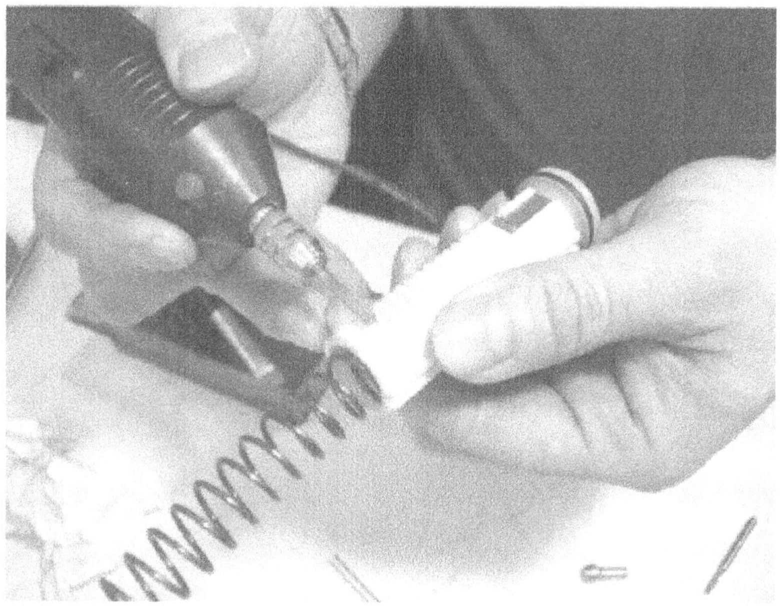

There are several parameters you want to know concerning piston quality. A pistons lateral movement is restricted by its guide rails, so if the guide rails are not made with precise dimensions and smooth surfaces then problem can occur. "tighter" rails can restrict piston movement, while "looser" rails may lead to unexpected issues.

The Effective teeth height is the measurement of how far the main teeth on a piston meshes into the sector gear. Some pistons have teeth which meshes too deep thus produces problems with the sector gear.

Full rack excursion measures how far back the piston is pulled on a full sector gear rotation. A piston which is pulled further back can exhibit slightly higher FPS and can give the system a slightly longer time to load the BBs.

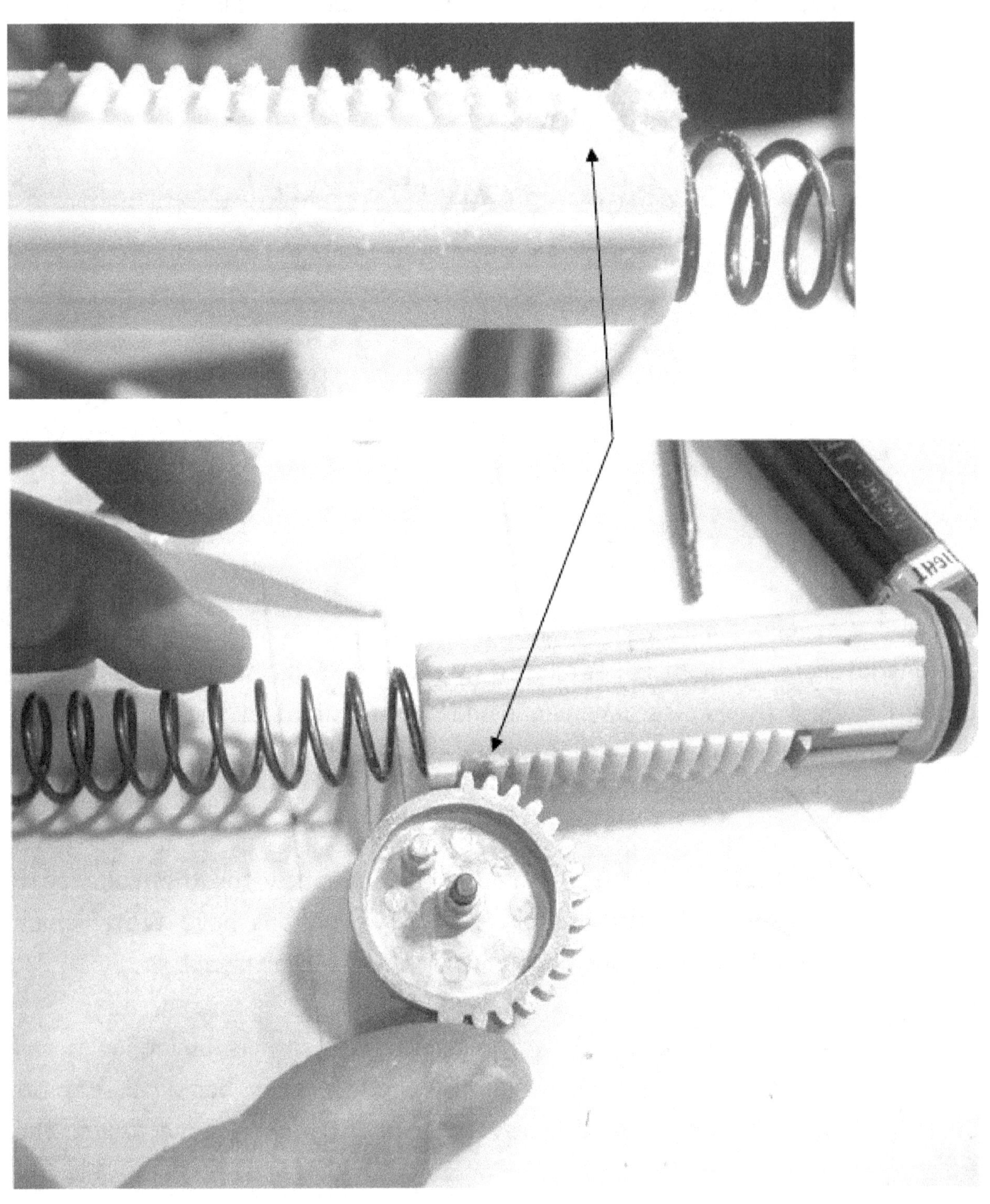

Some pistons use metal teeth only. These pistons tend to be more durable, but at the expense of weight.

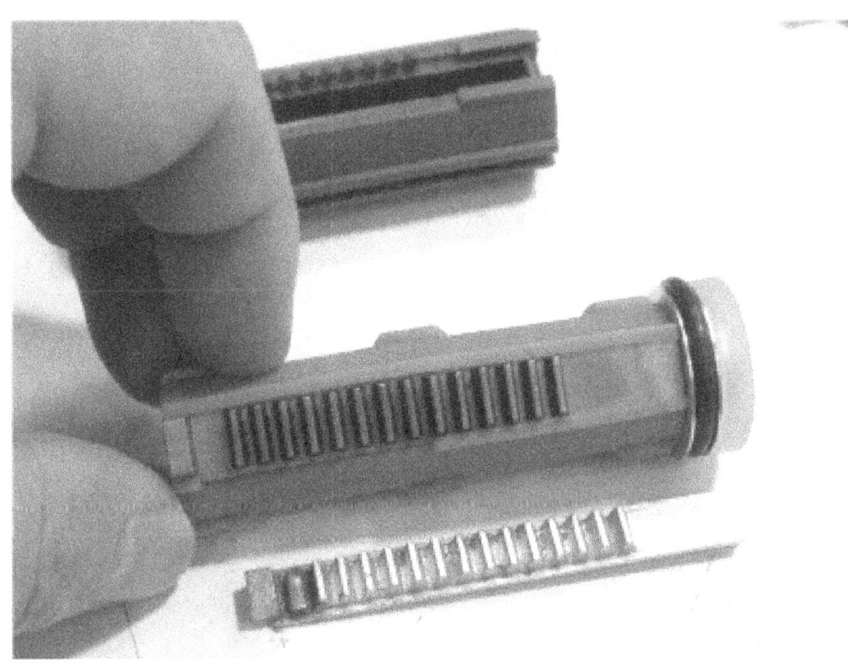

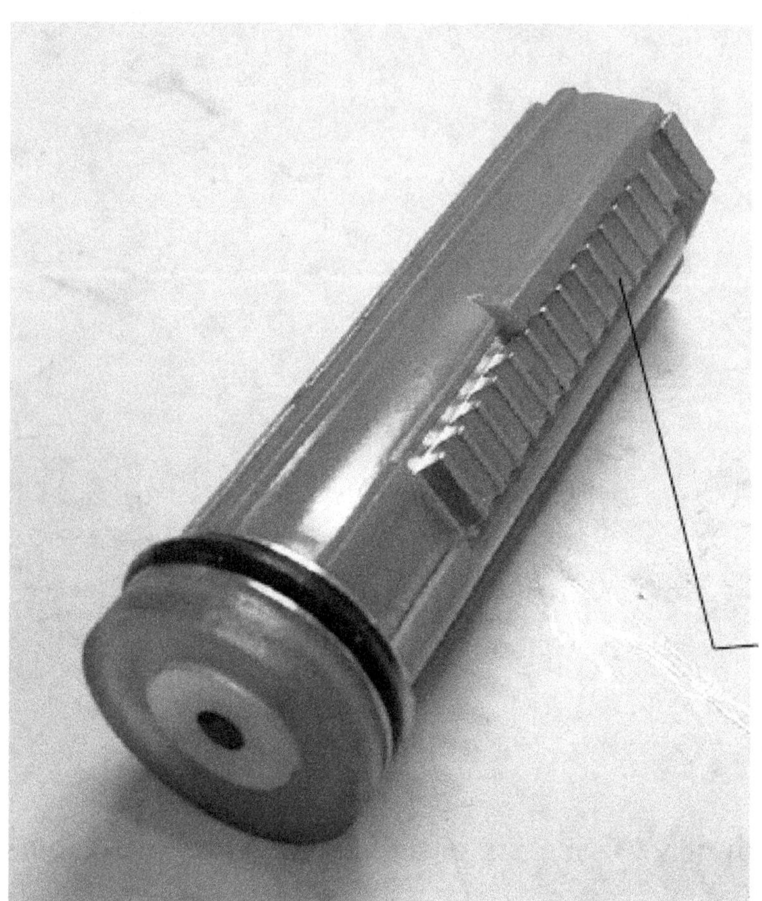

The metal teeth can be detached from the piston body.

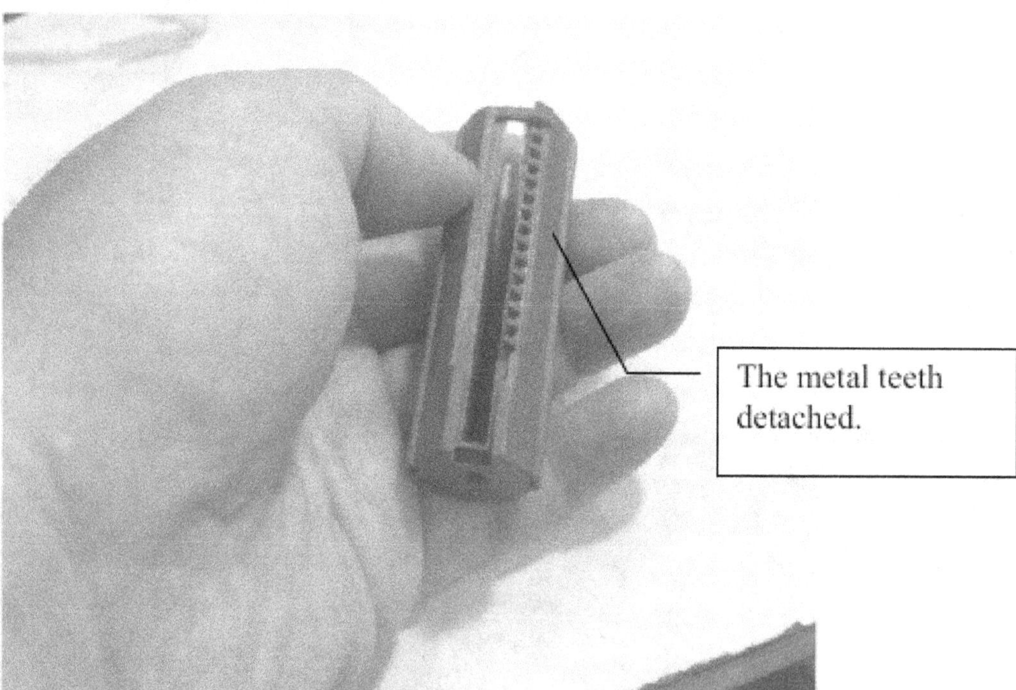

The metal teeth detached.

The piston head is the component that hits the cylinder head when the spring pushes the piston to the fullest extent. Both of them must be strong or they will not survive the impact.

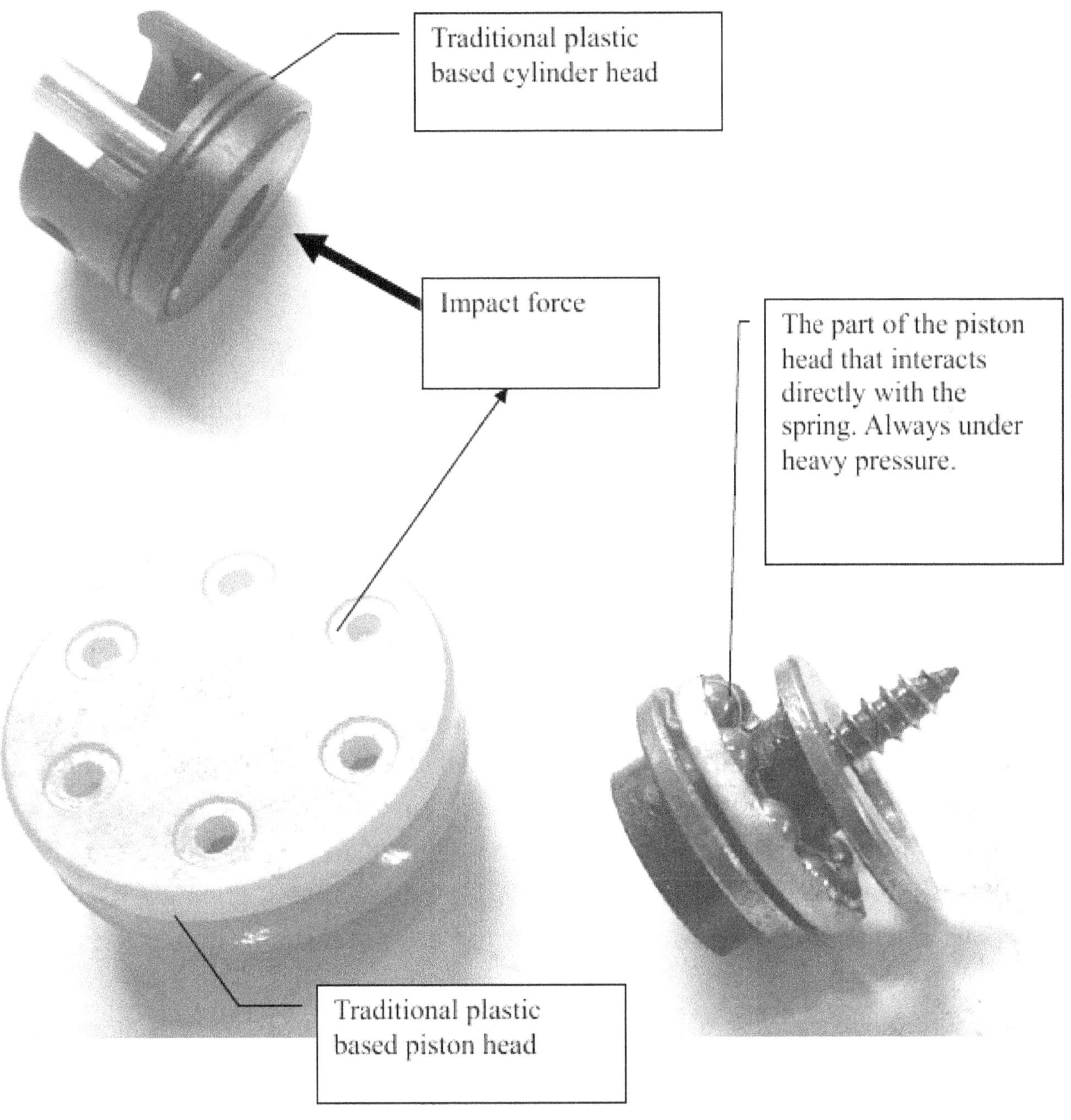

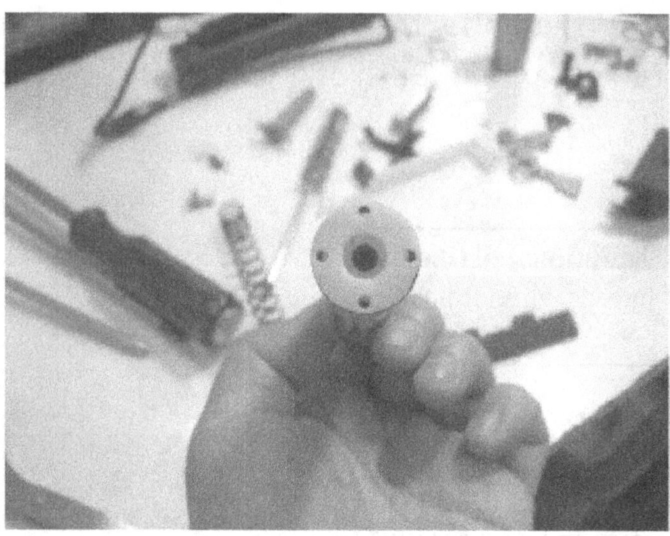

Upgraded piston heads usually have holes on the front face of the head. When the piston is moving forward, air goes through these holes and forces the surrounding O-ring outwards to create a seal for preventing air leakage.

The holes do not have to be big. A diameter of 0.18~0.2 inch will do just fine. The number and position of the holes do matter. You want to have at least 4 holes, and based on our experience there is no need to have more than 8 holes.

We do not see any reason why you should use a metallic piston head. The stock piston head is good at absorbing much of the impact generated by the spring on the gearbox shell. You should not need to replace the piston head unless the stock one breaks or that a bore-up cylinder is to be used. The replacement piston head does not have to be a metallic one though.

A silent head set has a bumper-rubber installed in both the cylinder head and piston head. While it can reduce noise a little bit, beware that noise also come from the other parts of the gearbox and also from the motor. You need custom works on the gun to achieve total noise reduction.

The latest trend of the airsoft industry is to go high tech! There are electronic trigger switch that replaces the traditional AEG contact switch. There are electronic switches for V3 gearbox, suitable for use with AK and Galil. They are not cheap, but they add program-ability to your AEG.

The ASCU Airsoft Smart Control Unit is a FET based "smart device" that can be installed onto the gearbox equipped with strong magnet motor. It monitors triggering and guarantees full cycle. Simply put, it improves trigger response and provides support for burst mode firing. Some wiring has to be done for it to work. It works using kind of a "push button" mechanism internally. Every cycle the "push button" is "pushed" to record a full cycle.

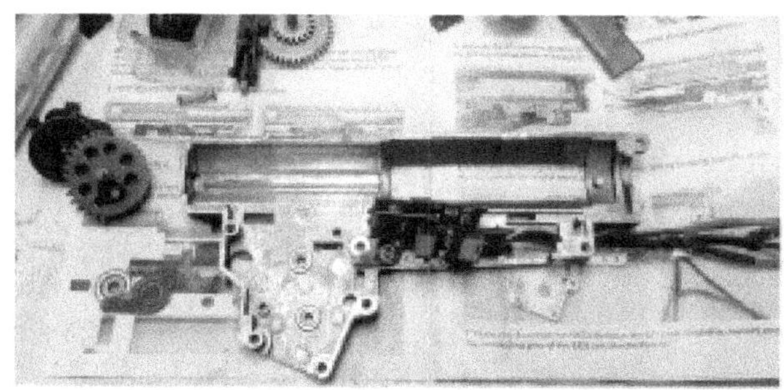

The KG9 gearbox is similar to a V3. The ASCU unit can fit in but some minor modifications on the gearbox shell are necessary.

REVIEW QUESTIONS AND ANSWERS

Question 1:

Refer to the photo below:

What gear drives this component?

A. sector
B. bevel
C. spur
D. pinion
E. None of the choices are correct.

Question 2:

Refer to the photo below:

This component directly drives which gear?

A. sector
B. bevel
C. spur
D. pinion
E. None of the choices are correct.

Question 3:

Refer to the photo below:

This component is for supporting:

A. the air nozzle
B. the cylinder
C. the piston
D. the spring
E. None of the choices are correct.

Question 4:

Refer to the photo below:

The highlighted component is for:

A. hopup release
B. safety switch
C. cosmetic purpose
D. body takedown
E. bolt locking
F. None of the choices are correct.

Question 5:

Refer to the photo below:

What is the highlighted component for?

A. safety
B. select fire
C. mag drop
D. hopup adjustment
E. pulling the nozzle
F. None of the choices are correct.

Question 6:

Refer to the photo below:

Refer to the highlighted gear. What gear is this?

A. spur
B. bevel
C. sector
D. reversal
E. None of the choices are correct.

Question 7:

Identify this component:

A. Piston
B. Spring guide
C. Air nozzle
D. Receiver pin
E. Motor adjustment screw
F. None of the choices are correct.

Question 8:

Identify this component:

A. Sector gear
B. Delayer
C. Bevel gear
D. Spur gear
E. Anti-reversal
F. None of the choices are correct.

Question 9:

Identify this component:

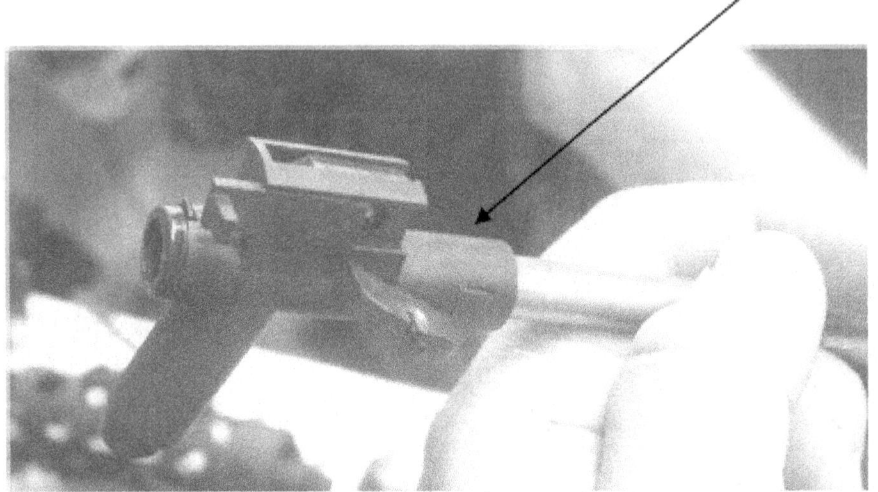

A. Mag catch
B. Spring release
C. Anti-reversal
D. Delayer
E. Battery compartment cover
F. Hopup unit
G. None of the choices are correct.

<u>Answers</u>

1. A
2. B
3. D
4. B
5. E
6. B
7. E
8. D
9. F

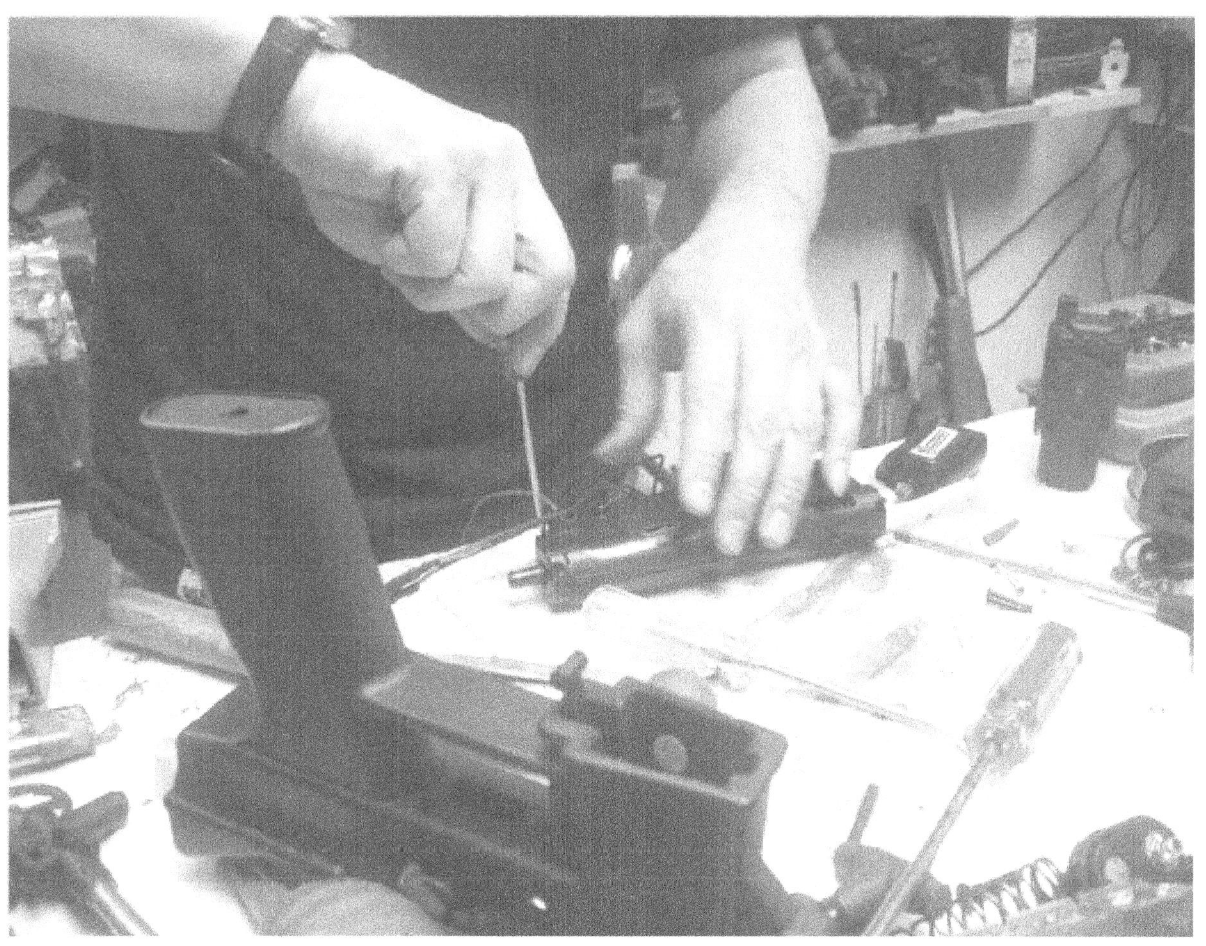

CONCLUSION

Thank you for completing this self paced training module. The module gives you a clear and concise introduction to the different performance elements of the KG9 AEG.

For latest product releases, updates and other free resources such as tech tips and InfoAPPS, please visit **http://airsoftpress.com**

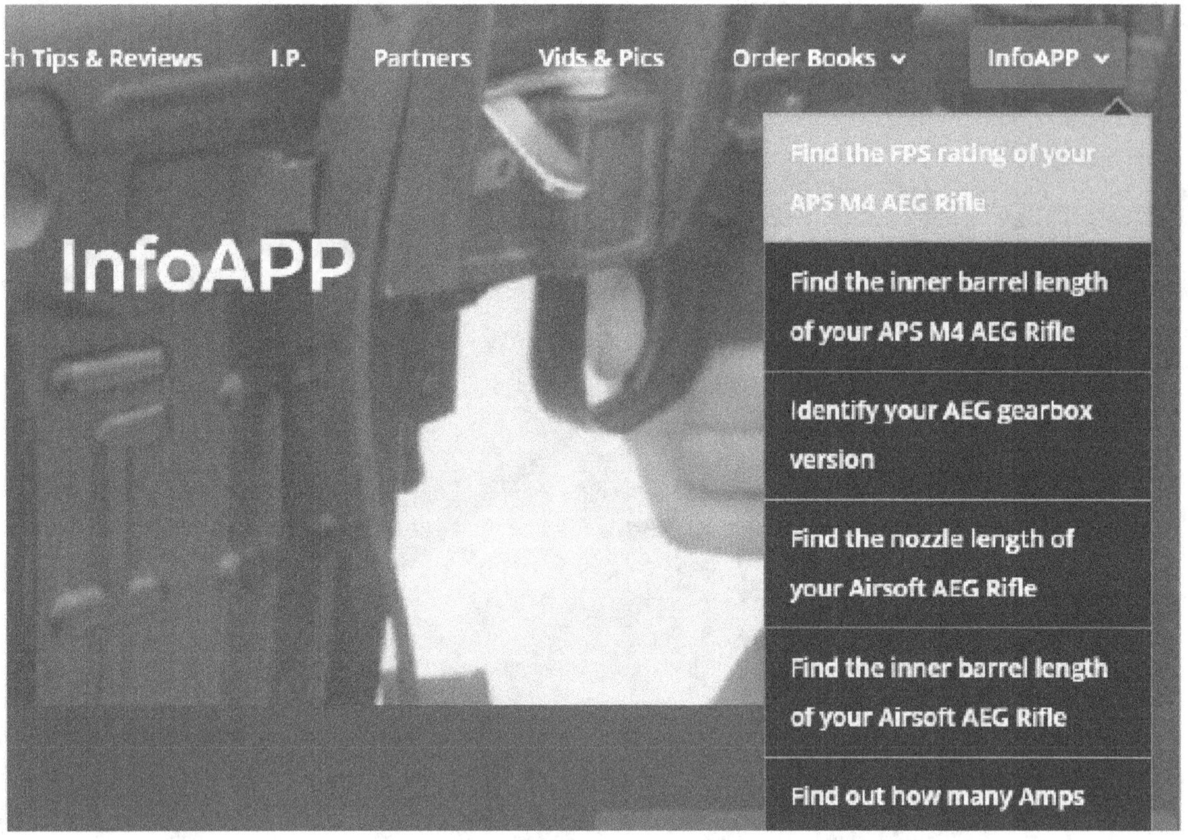

Please email your questions and comments to editor@airsoftpress.com.

Thank you.

